When the Kids Come First

Enhancing Self-Esteem

When the Kids Come First

Enhancing Self-Esteem

James A. Beane
&
Richard P. Lipka

Educator's International Press, Inc.
Troy, NY

Beane, James A. & Lipka, Richard P.
When the Kids Come First

Published by Educator's International Press, Inc.
18 Colleen Road
Troy, N.Y. 12180

Previously published by National Middle Schools Association © 1987

Library of Congress Cataloging-in-Publication Data:

Beane, James A., 1944-
    When the kids come first: enhancing self-esteem
       James A. Beane & Richard P. Lipka   p. cm.
    Includes bibliographical references.
    ISBN 1-891928-07-4 (pbk. : alk. paper)

    1. Self-esteem—Study and teaching (Middle school) 2. Self-esteem in children. 3. Self-perception in children. 4. Middle schools—Curricula. I. Lipka, Richard P. II. Title.

LB1117.B39 2000   99-088512
    370.15'3—dc21

Manufactured in the United States of America

05 04 03 02 01 00   1 2 3 4 5 6

Dedication

To the memory of R. Stewart Jones, Professor of Educational Psychology, University of Illinois-Urbana-Champaign. Stew's life as a university educator epitomized all the characteristics and qualities discussed in this book. He accepted all students as worthwhile human beings regardless of their background. He relished the diversity of individual differences and was a shining beacon to minorities, international students, and folks who marched to the tune of a different drummer. Stew opened his heart and home to his students with the expectation that they would do the same so that he might learn about their lives outside of the classroom. All of us who knew Stew came away with a clearer understanding and more positive view of ourselves as people and educators.

What Difference Would it Make?

**If we know that
young adolescents . . . and . . . we don't . .**

—Often are unhappy about their physical appearance

—offer opportunities to learn about variability in physical development, to develop good nutritional habits, or to control some physical developments through hygiene and exercise.

—want to make social connections and earn status with peers

—use group learning techniques, assist learning of social interaction skills, and provide opportunities to demonstrate individual skills and talents in project situations.

—are seeking initial independence, yet need security

—provide guidance programs, involve learners in decision making, or encourage individual interests.

—are moving toward formal operational thought

—accept the need for individualization, educate parents about transescent characteristics and recognize the need for flexibility with structured guidelines.

—are confused about dawning sexuality

—explain sexual development, discuss value issues associated with sexual activity, and help in exploration of sex roles.

—desire a sense of commitment as a source of self-worth

—arrange for peer tutoring, sponsor community service project programs or discuss social problems in this and other parts of the world.

—are confused about the ambiguities in our society

—provide opportunities to study contemporary media and its effects on self-images, accept diverse family patterns, and demonstrate reasonably stable adult role models.

—are experimenting with self-image roles

--encourage acceptance of diversity and respect the roles they try out.

--seek affection, self-respect, and dignity

—learn their names, ask about their personal interests, accept them unconditionally as human beings, and learn to laugh with them.

—often question their abilities in school

—communicate positive expectations and point out those things, no matter how small, which they do well.

—are in the process of growing and developing

—provide an environment which recognizes that the process of growing up is the process of making mistakes.

Contents

Foreword for 2000
A Message of Enduring Importance

More than 12 years have passed since *When the Kids Come First* was published by National Middle School Association. Many events in middle-level education have taken place since then. NMSA has grown from a fledgling professional association to become the leading national voice for middle-level education. Turning Points, the Carnegie Corporation's major report was published and gave middle-level education never-before-achieved visibility among the general public. The substantial support of several major foundations made possible a number of middle-level reform efforts across the nation. Almost every state has had its own middle-school initiative in the last decade. Professional resources for middle-level educators have expanded dramatically.

One might assume, then, that a 1987 publication would be dated and in need of major revision. Not so. Although remarkable progress has been made in organizing middle-level schools, the character of the curriculum and nature of the instructional practices employed in the typical middle-level classroom have changed little. In fact, the obsession with test scores has led to some regression in the ways young adolescents are taught. Regrettably, calls for accountability—as measured by inadequate and unfair tests—have stalled many significant reform efforts initiated by pioneering middle-school teachers in the 70s and 80s. Needed even more than ever are schools that respect students as important persons rather than pawns in a narrow process of schooling that rises and falls on the basis of paper and pencil test scores.

This volume crystallized many of the beliefs of leading middle-level educators when it was first published. It gave voice to the unapologetic, child-centered philosophy that was responsible for much of the early success of middle-level education. Reading *When the Kids Come First* again makes me realize how timeless its message is and how sad that it has not been more widely implemented in the ways middle schools actually operate. Yet, I am not discouraged; for there always has been a core of educators whose educational advocacies are built on what is known about human growth and development, the principles of learning, and whose commitment to democracy as a way of life has never flagged. And at this chronologically prime time I believe that cadre is growing and will lead in making the basic changes desperately needed. The serious limitations of traditional schools are becoming obvious. The times demand a real and personal education for all students, not simply a narrow schooling that perpetuates passive learning and does as much to sort and select as it does to truly educate.

My hope is that the sound and valid viewpoints presented in this volume will receive a fair and wide hearing, that policy makers and educational leaders will be led to put aside old, false assumptions about soft pedagogy or watered-down curriculum and recognize the truths presented here, ones that will lead to increased achievement and more ethical citizens. Until students are more actively involved in their own education, until they experience democracy in the classroom, until they are recognized as worthy adults in the making, until they see inherent meaning in their schoolwork, we will be unable to advance this great society of ours that is now experiencing frightening assaults from within.

John H. Lounsbury
December 1999

Foreword

Middle school educators tend to talk and write a lot about the importance of helping early adolescents develop positive self-concepts. Rare is the school philosophy or statement of goals that does not give specific attention to this intention. But when teachers and administrators get down to "brass tacks" and start planning schedules, determining curriculum, and selecting materials, the development of pupils' self-esteem usually takes a back seat. The unstated but prevalent assumption is that such a concern will take care of itself if we organize a "good" school.

The well-established rituals and routines of schooling then take hold and soon everyone is busy operating the institution. The time-honored practices relating to grouping, grading, and covering content inevitably, it seems, rule the day. And while teachers are conscientious and understanding, the "system" seems to master them and restrict their actions directed toward supporting students' personal development to the occasional comment squeezed into a day of controlling, instructing, and testing.

This monograph, if read and reacted to as it should be, will all but eliminate any such passing over of direct concern for this critical matter of enhancing students' self-esteem. Anyone who comes to grips with this aspect of middle-level education, as Beane and Lipka have made it possible to do with this publication, simply cannot, I believe, ignore it at decision-making time. Business as usual is not acceptable if we really care about kids and put them, as we should and this monograph's title proclaims, first. A true middle school must be able to point to its direct, intentional efforts designed to enhance the self-esteem of pupils. Enhancing self-esteem is a basic responsibility of middle-level schools. It is, in the words of the authors, "a compelling moral imperative."

The opening chapter of the publication makes a strong case for the imporatnce of self-perception, and sets forth a rational specifically focused on early adolescents that is based on history, contemporary issues, and solid research. Any studied reflection on the nature and needs of early adolescents will result in a recognition that the concerns of this age groups, whether we like it or not, are more social, emotional, and physical than intellectual. No middle school can be effective academically that does not acknowledge the impact of the developmental tasks transescents are undergoing. The self-concept effects and is very much affected by all aspects of their development.

Transescents are persons first. students.second. Their personal agendas and the school's agenda are only occasionally correlated. Even those educators whose nearly exclusive educational priorities center around the cognitive domain will find the achievement of their ends is most likely to be attained if the school gives direct attention to the business of helping transescents develop positive self-esteem.

What is advocated here is no narrow, simplistic program, no series of "lessons" on self-concept, but rather a school in which kids come first, where the genuine needs of transescents are the basics for decisions. This realistic and courageous statement is not a call for a few "warm fuzzies." It is, rather a case for a deeply rooted, widely practiced humaneness, a posture that is taken not just because it makes kids feel good but because it is directly related to increased achievement and the other objectives of middle-level education.

Would that we could make every middle-level school a self-enhancing school in which kids "grow positively in an understanding of themselves, their values, their social relationships, and the world in which they find themselves." Here is a tool that will make a major contribution to bringing such schools into existence. Take it, familiarize yourself with it, share it with other educators and parents, and use its contents as guides when plans are made about the kinds of educational experiences transescent youth will experience.

John H. Lounsbury
Editor, NMSA Publications

INTRODUCTION

For more than two decades the middle school has been the focus of one of the truly authentic reform movements in the history of education. The astonishing aspect of this movement is not the increasing number of "middle schools," but the willingness of educators at this level to seriously think about the function and form of these schools. Unlike so many other reform efforts this one has given considerable attention to learners rather than special interests outside the school. No matter what the reasons for reorganization at the local level, most participants have come to know the litany of characteristics associated with emerging adolescence or, more technically, "transescence."

Hardly a book, article, or speech about middle schools goes by that does not first recite that litany. When the infrequent exception occurs, the authors or speakers are expected to weave such information into whatever programs they recommend so as to justify their ideas. These expectations have resulted in continuing pressure for more information about transescence. And so we have come to know more and more about the physical, cognitive and socio-emotional characteristics and needs of this stage of development. This volume is an attempt to add to the portrait of transescence. Its focus is on the particular characteristics of self-concept and esteem and how middle schools might enhance them.

In one sense we began this work in 1975 with a paper about self-concept and self-esteem at the annual conference of the National Middle School Association. Since then we have done research on this phenomenon across all school levels. However, we have continued to keep transescence at the top of the agenda because our work and that of others reveal that this developmental stage is a critical juncture in the dynamic flow of self-perceptions. Also, educators at the middle level, perhaps sensing this, have shown greater interest in this topic than those at other levels.

In the pages that follow we paint a picture of what we have come to call a self-enhancing school. *A self-enhancing school is one which helps young people to clarify their self-concepts, develop positive self-esteem, formulate values, and understand their relationship to the social world around them. A self-enhancing middle school is one which helps transescents do these things.* Developing such a school requires that several questions be addressed. How do self-perceptions appear in the transescent stage? How do they function in relation to life inside and outside the school? What factors influence how transescents view themselves? How can the school and its programs be organized so as to enhance self-concept and esteem; what might be effective institutional features, appropriate curriculum arrangements, and premium teaching techniques? It is these questions which this volume seeks to answer.

By way of introduction, one other item needs to be mentioned. Our work has been guided by the idea that if one wants to know about young people's self-perceptions it is probably better to ask them directly than to make inferences from behaviors or from standardized instruments which reflect adult values — especially in transescence when the gap between youth and adult agendas often yawns so wide and surface behaviors may reveal little of what is felt inside. So, in the Spring of 1986 as we undertook this writing we began by asking two groups of transescents, one in Kansas and one in New York, to answer a series of questions about their self-images in school. In this way we hoped to gain some fresh insights or a least to have our old ones verified. These young people worked in groups so as to reflect some interaction on their part regarding our questions. Thus enlightened we felt more confident than ever in seeing this project through. Beyond that result we were also impressed again at how willing they are to help and how seriously they work when the task at hand touches personal aspects of their lives. And we continue to be firm in our belief that when adults ask young people to talk about themselves in school, it is almost impossible to forget that they are people first and students only after that.

Chapter 1

The Case for Enhancing
Self-Perceptions

Since the early 1970's there has been a steady push for increasing the role of academic rigor in the schools. Fueled by the media, pushed by federal and state officials, and supported by some educators this trend has narrowed the scope of elementary school programs to simple cognitive achievement and increased the academic requirements for high school graduation. It has led to curriculum mandates which amount to little more than covering content, but enough content to strangle the affective programs of many schools.

At the same time, the middle school movement has come of age, now approaching three decades of effort to reconstruct both organization and programs to better meet the needs of transescents. Many middle schools have managed to strike a well-planned balance between academic and affective concerns, but their work is now at risk. The obsession with recall and recognition of simple cognitive outcomes at the elementary level has been pushed up into the middle level and the requirements of the high school forced down. Many middle level advocates are now scrambling to hold together the integrity of their programs and a few have been beaten into submission. Yet the vast majority still know that the issues of transescence are largely affective and that a middle school must have these issues on its agenda in order to be effective.

At the very heart of these affective concerns is the development of clear self-concept and positive self-esteem. These represent the central feature of the human personality which, in the case of transescents, brings together the physical, social, and cognitive characteristics into a sense of identity, adequacy, and affirmation. And from the sense of self springs a myriad of variables such as behavior, perceptions of others, and motivation. Understanding these things brings us closer to understanding transescents. Attending to them in school brings us closer to developing the kind of middle school transescents need and deserve.

Among middle school educators there are many who are aware of this logic but uncertain how to articulate it, others who perhaps have not thought about it, and a few who have heard it, yet remain unconvinced. Whichever the case, we believe that there are three main reasons which may be advanced to answer the question, "Why enhance self-perceptions in the middle school?" One argues from a historical perspective, a second from a moral imperative, and a third from

3

the growing body of research on self-concept and esteem. Somewhere among the three there ought to be something to persuade even the most reluctant among us.

An Historical Precedent

In the early part of this century a new kind of school called a junior high school was established. Among the reasons used to support its existence was that it would have a program appropriate to the characteristics and needs of early adolescents (Melton, 1984). One means for achieving that goal was provision for a guidance program, although originally the emphasis was on vocational guidance since many youth left school after completing the junior high years. In time, however, the purpose of the guidance component was expanded. Listen to Gruhn and Douglass in 1947.

> *Guidance in Personal Development.* Guidance, like exploration, is as old as the junior high school itself. In fact, guidance was one of the functions most often emphasized in the early literature urging the development of junior high school programs. However, like exploration, the concept of guidance has been considerably broadened since the first junior high schools were introduced. In the beginning, vocational and educational guidance were particularly emphasized, because of the large number of drop-outs during the junior high school years. This situation has changed greatly.
>
> In place of emphasis on vocational guidance, there has been much more attention in the junior high school to helping pupils with personal, social, and emotional problems. It is only natural that this development should have taken place. In the past twenty-five years we have learned much about the psychological, physiological, and emotional development of young adolescents. In recent years, numerous books have been written on mental health and its relation to the educational program. The implications of these writings have been particularly significant for the junior high school grades. As a result, guidance in the junior high school today is directed toward helping boys and girls with all the problems and adjustments that they face. These include problems dealing with their educational progress, social development, emotional growth, and adjustments to new situations.

Two decades later Alexander and his colleagues (1968) expanded the idea of guidance even further in defining "personal development" as one of the components of a middle school curriculum. In their description of this area, they provided many examples of possible activities, including some which would occur in regular classroom settings.

This cursory look at the history of guidance in the middle level school suggests that guidance in terms of personal and social growth has always had a place at this level. This function was not relegated to a guidance department alone, although such services were to be incuded. Rather "guidance" was to be a function which permeated the entire school and its implementation was to be a responsibility of all personnel. As such the middle level school was often referred to as a "guidance school." Even the advisory programs of which we are so proud today are really variations on the classic "home-base" and "core" programs.

The idea of promoting personal and social growth, including enhancement of self-concept and self-esteem is, therefore, not new rhetoric conjured up by latter

4

day theorists. It is part of the history of middle level schools. Paying attention to self-perceptions in today's middle schools is part of the evolving effort to provide a balanced and complete education.

The Contemporary Scene

Attending to self-perceptions follows logically from the school's responsibility in promoting good mental health. Self-concept and esteem are central features in the human personality. When clear and positive they contribute not only to self-actualization, but also to constructive behavior in social interactions. On the other hand, unclear or negative self-perceptions contribute to debilitating behaviors both personally and in social settings.

We live in troublesome times. Ours is a world of ambiguity and ambivalence, of discontinuity and disbelief. The old order is breaking up not only in the industrial to post-industrial economic shift, but in the lifestyles we choose and the diversity of values we espouse. A quick glance around shows us that many adults are having a hard time finding anything to hang onto. For the young, whose life skills are not so mature, the scenario is even more complicated. Traditional sources of stability such as family, the church, the legal system, and even the prospects for eventual employment are rapidly shifting. The only certainty is uncertainty.

What must it be like to view this world through the eyes of an eleven or twelve or thirteen year old? How must it feel to try to find a place in a world where change is the rule of the day? Where can one find affirmation when traditional support systems have turned to criticism of youth and sometimes selective ignorance of their needs? And so we see among many youth increased incidence of drug use, eating disorders, early pregnancy, crime activity, and attempted and actual suicide. Some say these are signs of anarchy in youth — how sad and misguided a view. Instead these are symptoms of loss of self-worth, of loss of social place, of unclear values.

Meanwhile, other groups prey upon the transescents' search for identity and need for self-esteem. For example, commercial media and the Madison Avenue image makers suggest paths to self-fulfillment and social status, but they are often only cosmetic changes and quick-fix solutions — as if self-perceptions existed on the outside instead of within the human make-up. If self-esteem or self-satisfaction is represented in the difference between the ideal self (what I wish I was) and the real self (who I actually am), then it is possible also to begin to feel the discomfort and dissonance transescents may experience when confronted with commercial messages.

The point of all this is that constructing clear self-concepts and positive self-esteem is difficult enough even without the mixed messages in today's social scene. In fact, we believe that it is generally much more difficult to grow up in today's world than it was only a generation or two ago. Louis Raths once said that "the process of growing up is the process of making mistakes," but today as never before the risks are greater, the stakes higher. For many transescents the school has become a kind of Maginot Line or place of last resort in their lives. The middle level school may be the last institution where these young people may work with a group of adults who, as Raths said, are willing to "give them help and guidance,

5

not just criticism.'' In this sense, then, we may argue the case for self-concept and esteem in the school as a compelling moral imperative. Such work has to do with more than just the school; it has to do with the larger life outside as well.

Reasons from Research

Many people today are not interested in historical or moral reasoning when it comes to education. Instead they want someone to tell them about research-based reasons for doing anything beyond mastery of basic content or skills. For those who fall in this group, there is another argument for attending to self-concept and esteem in school.

The fact is that there have been literally hundreds of studies done on self-perceptions. Most of those have involved self-concept or esteem in young people and most of these have looked partially or wholly at the relationships between various dimensions of self-perceptions and desired outcomes in school. Of this last group, a substantial number have looked at such correlations as they develop in middle level schools or as they evolve across several grades including those found at the middle level.

When one reads through research on the relationship between self-perceptions and school success, some consistent patterns emerge. Apparently, those young people with clear self-concepts and positive self-esteem tend to do better on a number of school variables than those whose self-perceptions are confused and negative. Following are some examples of the findings.

Participation: If a learner has negative self-esteem, he or she is likely, in pro-social situations, to avoid public notice and risk-taking: "If I think I am incompetent, why should I raise my hand and have the group think so too.'' A learner with positive self-esteem is likely to have confidence that supports displaying self in public, especially among peers. For this reason, those young people with positive self-esteem are more likely to participate in both classroom and other school activities.

School Completion: Learners with clear school related self-concepts and positive self-esteem see school as an important and success producing part of their lives. Those who are ambivalent about the value of school and/or have had repeated lack of success come to have negative school self-esteem. In general, the former tend to persist in school and develop life-long learning habits while the latter cases are more likely to drop out and/or see the ending of school as the ending of learning.

Social Status. Earning a place in the peer group is a compelling force in transescence. Thus when such a place is gained and status awarded, positive self-esteem results. Conversely, group rejection is a sure bet for negative self-esteem. However, it is also the case that positive and negative self-feelings are often projected on others and readily visible to them. This self and social interaction explains why those with positive self-esteem tend also to have social status among peers.

Behavior. As in the case of earning social status, positive and negative self-esteem enter into relations with others. Those with positive self-esteem tend to project that view into interactions in constructive ways while those with negative self-esteem seem frequently to be in conflict with both peers and adults. These cases are compounded by the tendency toward stability in self-views: persons with positive self-esteem tend to seek feedback from others which is favorable while those with negative self-esteem often act so as to receive negative feedback. In cases of cooperative versus conflict behavior in school, such differentiated feedback is almost guaranteed.

Self-Direction. When teachers assign independent work they are often confronted by one or two students who ask, repeatedly, "Is this what you want? Am I doing this right?" Most likely these learners are telling the teacher that they are unsure of themselves and lack self-confidence. Other students seem able to get to work and keep at the same assignment to its completion. These two cases illustrate the relationship between self-concept/esteem and the capacity for self-direction. Those whose self-perceptions are clear and positive tend to be more able to work independently while their peers with confused or negative self-perceptions generally lack the confidence to do so.

Achievement. Success in school, academically, socially and physically, is strongly related to self-concept and esteem. Those learners who feel clear and positive about themselves in school, especially with regard to the belief that they can succeed, tend to demonstrate consistent achievement. Those who have confused or negative self-views in school, particularly those who believe they cannot succeed, tend to experience low levels of achievement. These correlations appear persistently in research literature often at levels higher than those between intelligence and achievement (e.g. Brookover et al., 1964 and Purkey, 1970).

In the "worst case" scenario some learners come to believe that they cannot succeed in school no matter how hard they try; success is attributed to external factors (e.g. luck), while failure is seen as internal (e.g. lack of ability). When these feelings continue over time, they may result in "learned helplessness." Such students usually end up in remedial or learning disabilities classes, where such groupings may reinforce negative self-perceptions. It is important to know that learned helplessness tends to solidify between grades six and eight and limited progress is made thereafter even with special help (Bryan and Bryan, 1987).

Thus a compelling reason for enhancing self-concept and esteem in the middle school is the persistent results of research. Clearly, school success does not function in a vacuum. It is an effect which interacts with other variables, including self-perceptions. We are well aware that other factors like intelligence, socio-economic status and teaching behaviors also show up in school success studies. But, we are also increasingly convinced that when learners lose confidence in themselves or question their ability, such variables as intelligence tend to show diminished effects. At any rate, in this research-based argument those who are not given to historical or moral persuasion should find reason to be concerned about self-perceptions in school.

A Word More About Research on Self-Perceptions

Before leaving our brief look at research on self-perceptions and school success, it might be helpful to extend the comments on the meaning of that research. When interpreting the results of research such as that just described one must exercise some caution. First, the connection between self-concept/esteem and school variables has been substantiated as correlational, not casual. In other words, types of self-perceptions and various school attitudes and behaviors are found simultaneously in groups of learners, but we cannot be certain that the former *cause* the latter. This does not mean the casual relationships do not exist, as most of us believe intuitively; it is that such connections are just now beginning to show up in the research literature.

For this reason we view the relationship between self-perceptions and school variables in a cycle (see Figure 1). Self-concept/esteem interacts with school actions/behaviors, one perhaps leading to the other in various situations, and as a result the individual receives feedback which in turn influences the self-perceptions. When learners experience success they receive positive feedback which supports positive self-perceptions and continued success. Lack of achievement leads to negative feedback which is related to poor self-perceptions° and continued difficulty in school. The longer either type of cycle continues through specific cases of success or failure, the more stable it is likely to become, for better or worse.

A second caution has to do with the interpretation of any behavioral science research. Data are typically gathered from groups, hopefully large ones. Thus the results show the tendency of groups and may not apply to every individual within them. For this reason, educators can usually name one or two exceptions to even the strongest research findings. Some, however, mistakenly use these to reject wholly such findings.

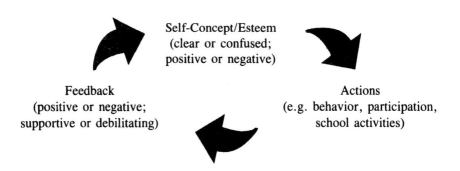

Self-Concept/Esteem
(clear or confused;
positive or negative)

Feedback
(positive or negative;
supportive or debilitating)

Actions
(e.g. behavior, participation,
school activities)

Figure 1.1. The Cycle of Self-Perceptions In School

A third caution, and reminder, is that self-concept and esteem tend to function in multi-dimensional and situation specific ways. Correlations are strongest between achievement in specific areas (e.g. mathematics or social status) and self-concept in those same specific areas. In other words, achievement in physical tasks correlates strongly to self-concept in physical tasks, but weakly to self-concept as math student. And, achievement in any given area would correlate more strongly to self-concept in that area than to general self-concept and esteem. Thus, when we attempt to use the self-concept/achievement connection with learners we must use clear, structured, and situation specific feedback. Telling an individual that he or she is a nice person will probably not go far in promoting positive attitudes in science, and, fortunately, criticizing a student in an academic subject will not necessarily debilitate social self-esteem. Again, following the lead of research, when we work with self-perceptions, we must concentrate on promoting success in specific areas.

Finally, in developing this monograph we have not relied only on our research. Instead, where various studies are cited in support of ideas they reflect the weight of the evidence found in reviews of many related studies, meta-analyses of research, or particular studies which involved large samples, careful procedures, and clear findings.

Self-Perceptions In School

In the laudable desire to have quick solutions for important and pressing problems many people think about enhancing self-concept and self-esteem in school as residing in once a week twenty minute group discussion of self and peer feelings. Others imagine an hour set aside every other Friday for doing one or two prescribed activities from one of the "how to" self-concept books. Still others speak of enhancing self-perception only in reference to improving academic achievement. The types of activities first mentioned do have a place in an overall scheme for enhancing self-perceptions, and so does the link with academic achievement. However, at best these views are short term and incomplete. They do not fill the bill for really supporting personal-social growth of transescents.

What is needed instead is a broader view in which concern for self-perceptions is seen to permeate the entire program of the school in both the explicit and hidden curriculum. That fact that such a view is not extraordinary is supported by the appearance in most school goal lists of at least one which speaks to "developing self-esteem" or "developing a sense of self-worth." Unfortunately, such a single goal is often too broad or ambiguous to suggest direction for school programs. We would recommend that middle school efforts to enhance self-perceptions be guided by such broad goals but clarified through five general objectives and related clarifying statements as follows:

1. Develop clear and accurate self-concept
   - recognizes personal strengths and limitations
   - applies self-evaluation skills adequately
   - is able to describe self without difficulty

2. Develop constructive values as sources of positive self-esteem
   - has clear values and beliefs
   - respects dignity of self
   - is concerned for welfare of others
   - listens to views of others and is open to new ideas
   - thinks carefully about value issues

3. Understands importance of self-perceptions in living and learning
   - knows that positive self-esteem is a key factor in self-respect
   - understands that positive self-esteem leads to satisfaction with life

9

- is able to envision satisfactory life plans
- strives for mental health

4. Develop skills for self-evaluation
   - knows techniques for self-assessment
   - adequately applies self-evaluation techniques
   - demonstrates continuous self-assessment
   - recognizes personal strength as well as limitations

5. Understands physical, social, and cognitive changes and how they affect self-perceptions
   - accurately describes stage developments in transescence
   - accepts reality and inevitability of transescent stage developments
   - accurately describes developments in childhood and adolescence
   - knows difference between controllable and uncontrollable events in transescence
   - recognizes that peers deal with similar events and concerns

Helping transescents to achieve these goals is a complex process. As mentioned before it is not likely to be done through small increments unrelated to the larger school program and it extends beyond academic achievement. The larger questions are these:

How can the features of the middle school as an institution be arranged so as to enhance self-perceptions?

How can the curriculum be organized to contribute to enhanced self-perceptions?

What can professionals such as teachers, administrators, and counselors as well as parents do to enhance self-perceptions?

10

Chapter 2
Self-Perception in Transescence

Those who work with, live with, or study transescents generally recognize that this is the most dramatic period of development in the human lifespan with regard to the breadth of change it involves. The physically underdeveloped child becomes the well-developed adolescent complete with secondary sexual characteristics, a voice an octave lower, and an adult-like shape, but not without the unpredictable and troublesome growth spurts, embarrassing acne, cracking voice, and loss of coordination in transescence. The adult-dependent, easily directed child becomes the self-assured, social adolescent but not without the drama of role-trying, peer obsession, and parental conflict in transescence. The reality-based child becomes the value and concept seeking adolescent, but not without the gray-area questioning and incomplete logic in transescence.

In short, the physical, social and cognitive adolescent is a much different person from the child before transescence. Since the self-concept consists largely of perceived images of those developmental characteristics, transescence may be viewed as a time when the self-concept undergoes virtual reconstruction. Moreover, based upon those changing images and shifts in value orientation, the self-esteem or degree of self-satisfaction is also open to extensive re-examination. It is to those issues, self-concept and self-esteem, that we now turn.

SELF-CONCEPT AS A SELF THEORY

The transescent, as with any other individual, is in the process of constructing an implicit theory about him/herself. While disagreement exists, nearly a century of theory building and research offers some fairly clear and consistent ideas about the content of self-theory. (e.g. James, 1890; Cooley, 1902; Snygg and Coombs, 1949; Rogers, 1951; Sullivan, 1953; Allport, 1955; Wylie, 1961, 1979; Kelley, 1962; Coopersmith, 1967; Gorden 1968; Gergen, 1971; Epstein, 1973; Rosenberg, 1979; Beane and Lipka, 1980, 1984; Lipka, Beane and Ludewig, 1980; Brinthaupt and Lipka, 1985a, 1985b; Lipka and Brinthaupt, 1986)

Levels Of Self-Perception

The construction and operation of our self-theory takes place at three levels: specific situation, category/attributes, and general. Each transescent in his or her daily life engages in specific situations e.g. physical education class, lunch room

11

discussions, problem solving activities in classes, and so on, through which he or she exercises and develops knowledge, skills, attitudes, beliefs. Each of these specific situations has the consequence of providing the individual with feedback about self. This feedback may be normative, that is derived from others, or the feedback may be formulated personally, based on some criteria the individual has set for self. Internalized, these forms of feedback become part of the self and have great impact upon guiding the behavior of the transescent.

In short, we should not be surprised when the transescent who has had a dreadful swimming experience resorts to forging a note from parents in order to avoid the mandatory pool session in the physical education class. For that transescent "self as swimmer" is loaded with negative affect, and that young person will go to great lengths to avoid an experience that has the potential to confirm that view of self. By the same token, a young person successful with computers may try to structure every school experience around computers in order to gain the positive affect associated with "self as computer jock."

The second level at which self-perceptions function is the category/attribute level. Here the transescent formulates ideas about self based upon roles he or she possesses. Since individuals are able to simultaneously conceive of themselves in terms of both categories and attributes we are able to process the perception of "6th graders with fat thighs" as:

  category-role: 6th grader

  attribute-physical feature: fat thighs

Given the great variability in physical development of transescents the attribute level is a common descriptor of self in the middle school as exemplified by some of the comments offered to us by seventh graders in response to the question *Things you think about in school:*

  - worry about weight -

  - how big our feet are -

  - how we smell -

  - what we look like -

  - our appearance -

When these self-perceptions are tied to negative self-esteem, school activities (e.g. competitive athletics) that accentuate physical attributes have the potential to cast a pall on the school experience. The key to this level of functioning is the identification and utilization of categories and roles in the school planning process as manifested in the problems and needs approaches to curriculum development discussed in Chapter 4.

The third level of self-perception functioning is the general sense of self. At the general level, a transescent may say something like, "All things considered I am a likeable person" or "I am not much good for anything in school." This general sense of self is a personal meta-analysis of many specific situations and weighted in favor of those roles and attributes that are most valued.

For educators concerned with enhancing the self-perceptions of transescents, understanding the three part concept is important, particularly when it is recognized that as self-perceptions move from the specific toward the general they are increasingly resistant to change.

The transescent who says "I am not much good for anything in school" has based this judgment on the weight of the evidence from many specific situations that function as perceptual screens through which new situations are processed. A single episode of positive feedback should not be expected to influence the general sense of self, nor very generalized statements such as, "you're a good person, you shouldn't feel bad about yourself." In fact, a transescent with generalized negative self-esteem is liable to view the former statement as dishonest or another example of a teacher who doesn't know him, e.g. "If you really knew me you wouldn't say I am a good person."

What seems to be needed is a continuous series of specific situations in which positive feedback is received or, in the event previous situations were misinterpreted, a guided review of past experiences with help directed at reconstructing the individual's interpretation of feedback received.

A student who says "I am not much good for anything in school" requires the nurturing of a teacher who is willing to talk with that individual about past experiences and look for cases where the youngster was "good for something" in school. With that knowledge in hand, a teacher could plan, with the student, a series of experiences/activities in which success is probable and, once attained, help the student internalize the feelings of success and develop expectations for the same in the future.

Influences Upon the Self

Kelley (1962) and Mead (1934) suggested that the self develops almost entirely as a result of interactions with others. That is, self-assessments and self-values are made in terms of the standards, criteria and value systems provided by the society. This thinking implies that while both the environment and the individual play a part, the environment is the more powerful force. To economize and focus the environment, individuals pay most attention to "significant others." As a transescent operationalizes a role in a defined situation he/she receives feedback from others which may be used to modify the self theory. The revised or refined self-theory is then tested in new situations in a search for validating feedback from the environment.

It is with the onset of transescence that peers emerge as the litmus paper of life. Clothing, musical tastes, real and imagined relationships with the opposite sex are all tested through the peer group. The immediate circle of peers serves as the fuel for the comment "everybody has one" when a transescent is polled about a sweatshirt, record, or particular swiss watch by a caring teacher or economically harried parent. The frequency of phone rings becomes the barometer of evening home life and morning preparations for school.

To make matters even more exciting the emergence of the importance of the peer group coincides with a desire of the transescent to be removed from adult guidance of daily activities. The increased importance of peers coupled with a perceived decrease in importance of adults is the ideal chemistry to produce gray hair in the adults who reside within the sphere of influence of the transescent, especially those adults who deny or choose to ignore the power of the peers within this age group.

13

The Developing Self

While an individual's self-theory develops largely in a social context, the structure and content of the self-theory also depends upon developmental characteristics of particular stages of growth. That is, emerging physical, cognitive and affective characteristics direct and/or guide the interaction that an individual has with his or her environment. The developmental research to date (e.g. Rosenberg, 1979; Lipka, Beane and Ludewig, 1980; Brinthaupt and Lipka 1985a, 1985b; Lipka and Brinthaupt, 1986) suggests that with increasing age there is an increasing complexity of self-theorizing. Rosenberg (1979) summarized the trend by indicating that the younger child sees the self as something external and overtly revealed for all to see, while the older child describes self more in terms of internal, convertly-concealed attributes. Put another way, recent research (e.g. Brinthaupt and Lipka, 1985a, 1985b; Lipka and Brinthaupt, 1986) supports the view of an age related shift in self-perceptions from: "I am what I *own*" to "I am what I *do*" to "I am who I *am*". That is, in early childhood young people in response to the question "Tell me about yourself" say such things as "I own a red bike," "I own a football," "I have a puppy," etc. Older children talk about themselves in terms of "playing football," "making models," "working with puzzles," etc. And adolescents talk about themselves in terms of "being fair," "shy," "outgoing," "even tempered," etc.

Transescence marks the beginnings of the shift from "I am what I *do*" to "I am who I *am*." We see the doing stage when we ask this age group what school subjects they like and the typical responses are Industrial Arts, Home Economics, Typing, and Communications - subjects which involve hands-on, doing activities and ones that encourage or at least permit peers working with other peers. We see the emerging of the "I am who I *am*" stage when we ask this group about the changes they are going through at this time in their lives and they respond:
- becoming more responsible -
- confusion in deciding between kids or mature young adults -
- we've started to understand how quickly time passes -
- we no longer have all the answers, therefore we feel like we're missing something -.

It is probably safe to say that as the stage of "I am who I *am*" shows up so does "Why am I the way I am?" and "Why are you the way you are?" and "Why do we have to do this?" Transescence becomes the age of questioning, the age of *why*. Many adults see this as a pain in the neck, when in reality they should probably throw a party to celebrate the fact that this Freudian style of psychic functioning and introspection is most likely indicative of the onset of formal operations in the cognitive domain. One outcome of this is that for the transescent, sexual self-perceptions become issues of roles, actions, and interpersonal styles (again, power to the peer group) rather than purely concerns of physical descriptions.

Keep in mind, we are talking about the onset of formal operations not total immersion in the stage. It helps us understand better how the same young people who were euphoric at the sight of Bon Jovi and Madonna can turn right around and organize a petition campaign for Bob Geldorf as *Time's* "man of the year"

14

for his work with world hunger; and indicate that threat of nuclear war colors their thinking about movement into the "adult" grown-up society.

The young people themselves know full well that they have embarked upon this journey into formal operations as a number we interviewed said, "we are beginning to understand what we must do in life and who we want to be."

Self-Esteem: The Prime Mover

As Rosenberg (1979) has noted, few activities engage our lives so profoundly as the interactive process we call self-esteem. For example, a transescent might describe herself as "smart" and then go on to say that she is happy or unhappy about being "smart." The latter judgment is an indication of self-esteem since it indicates how the individual feels about the description. In other words, self-esteem involves the individual's sense of self-worth or self-regard manifested in a wide range of feelings and actions. Self-esteem judgments are based upon values or value indicators such as attitudes, beliefs or interests. Understanding the place of values and value indicators in the formation of self-perceptions is of particular importance, since it highlights the fact that self-judgment is personal and that inferring the self-esteem of transescents is a risky venture. Just how risky a venture was made clear to us in 1978 when we conducted a small pilot study in which we asked one hundred fifth and seventh graders to complete a revision of Coopersmith's Self-Esteem Inventory (SEI). The revision consisted of having each student indicate for each item whether they would like to "keep" or "change" the aspect of themselves or whether they "don't care"! In Coopersmith's (1967) original research young people who checked "like me" for the Item: "I play with children younger than myself" were inferred to have negative self-esteem. However, within the pilot study almost equal numbers of students responded "keep", "change" or "don't care" which led us to hypothesize in four areas of activity.

First, a "like me" response could reflect a close knit family or sibling responsibilities due to two parents working, double bussing schedules, etc. just as easily as negative self-esteem.

Second, a "like me" response could reflect geographical isolation, such that playing with any children requires playing with children younger than oneself.

Third, a "like me" response might be elicited from a task focused individual who wants to play football and seeks out all other individuals (e.g. younger, older, same age, male and female) who express a desire to play football.

Fourth, a "like me" response may indeed be reflective of negative "self as peer" self-esteem as suggested by Coopersmith. In sum, given the four hypotheses, inferring negative self-esteem could place your inference at risk seventy-five percent of the time.

It is the personal evaluation process or "self-esteeming" which lends the ideas of stability, consistency and enhancement to the self. While those self-judgments are personal, the yardsticks (values, value indicators) for making the judgments are not. Acquiring these yardsticks requires curriculum arrangements which promote the choosing-prizing-acting dimensions of the valuing process. Acquiring these yardsticks requires a school environment that signals a desire to have power over problems rather than power over people; and gives those signals through teacher-pupil planned experiences of problem finding, problem distillation and problem solving. In short, the school is a major laboratory in the defining, refining and revising processes associated with self-esteem.

Imaginary Audience and Personal Drama

The formation of self-concepts and the self-esteeming activities are "growth" processes and not "grim" processes. We are not endorsing a "storm and stress" viewpoint, rather we are trying to indicate that the transescent's self-images are malleable, open, and vulnerable with part of the vulnerability derived from the view that transescents subject themselves to the two great myths described by Elkind (1967). The first is the "imaginary audience," the belief that "everyone is watching me." This feeling of being on-stage serves as a backdrop for rules and regulations in the peer culture: wear only Nike (or is it Reebok?) sneakers, only Lee (or is it Levi?) jeans and avoid being pointed out as smart in class. Oddly enough it rarely occurs to most transescents that their peers also feel that they have been singled out under this spotlight.

The second myth is the "personal drama" and is divided into two parts. One is that something, whatever it is, "only happens to me...never to anyone else." We come upon the weeping transescent standing in front of a locker that refuses to open and we hear those words: "this doesn't work." We open the locker and then point down the hall to twenty more unfortunates, likewise standing and weeping before obstinate lockers. To our young friend, however, these twenty similarly plagued peers are invisible, or if they did exist, their lockers would mysteriously open with ease. The other part of the personal drama is no less a myth, but it is more problematic. It is heard in the insistence that this thing, whatever it is, "could happen to other people, but it could never happen to me." If we look at our schools, they are filled with prevention programs having to do with substance abuse, sexual activity, and so on. Most transescents can recite chapter and verse on the consequences of drug use, the dangers of venereal disease, and the problems of adolescent parenthood. Yet we see all around us continuing and even increasing cases of such activity. It is perhaps the case that many do those things, knowing the consequences, but firm in their belief "that this could never happen to me."

Such myths often persist into adulthood, but they are particularly powerful in the transescent years. To work with transescent self-perceptions in enhancing ways, means having to deal with these myths.

Summary

Holding mercury in your fingers may be the most apt metaphor for this age group. We have made the case here and in other writings (e.g. Beane and Lipka, 1986) that this age-group is one of acute vulnerability due to rapid and, for the individual, unpredictable changes in the intellectual, feeling and physical domains. The broad base of these changes literally mandates the transescent to undertake a re-thinking of self-perceptions in virtually all dimensions. This "re-thinking" for most is clearly a growth process - a process that can and should be nurtured by caring and understanding adults.

16

Chapter 3
Self Perceptions in School: Institutional Features

Curriculum consists of all the experiences of the learner under the auspices of the school. Learning is not confined to the classroom nor is it limited to the intentions described in curriculum documents such as course sylabii. Young people learn in hallways, on buses, on playgrounds, and in the principal's office. They learn from the expectations of teachers, from interactions with peers, and from ways in which they are treated as people and as students. It is in these settings and by these means that young people come to know something of themselves and their relationships to others. This is the hidden curriculum. What is learned here is more powerful than the lessons of the intended curriculum plans since this is the part which touches, most deeply, the self-perceptions, values, and attitudes of learners.

Let's face it, the middle school is an institution. No matter how you cut it, it is a centralized place, maintained by society, where groups of transescents are brought by law to be supervised and instructed by adults. Because it includes large groups of learners and because it has expectations from society and the profession, it must be organized in some way. The various means for doing this we call "institutional features." They are the structures which define and regulate day-to-day life in the school. Institutional features include such things as climate, decision-making processes, rules and regulations, reward and punishment systems, grouping, relations with the outside world, and morale. Institutions do not have to be bad places, but they can be. The way in which their features are planned and carried out may contribute to positive self-perceptions or they may debilitate self-worth. If you think this isn't so, just ask a few transescents to tell you what makes them feel good or bad about themselves in school, the content of courses, or the way they are treated as people.

Climate: What Kind Of Place Is This?

The self-enhancing middle school provides an environment which promotes individual dignity and personal adequacy. The climate of the school serves as a backdrop for everything else that happens within it. Researchers who study school climate describe two types: One is called *custodial* climate. It is characterized by concern for maintenance of order, preference for autocratic procedures, student stereotyping or labeling, punitive sanctions, moralizing by authorities, impersonalness, and emphasis on obedience. The other type is called *humanistic* climate. This one is characterized by preference for democratic procedures, high degrees of interaction, personalness, respect for individual dignity, emphasis on self-discipline, flexibility, and participatory decision-making. Rarely does one or the other type totally dominate a school and all the events within. Usually, though, schools do lean heavily in one direction or the other and one does not need to spend much time inside a school to figure out which one holds sway.

The descriptions of custodial and humanistic climates have obvious implications for self-concept and esteem and there is a good deal of research to support the role of school climate (e.g. Willower and Jones, 1963; Deibert and Hoy, 1977). Like the old saying "children learn what they live," those learners who are in schools with generally humanistic climates demonstrate higher degrees of self-actualization and self-regard than those in custodial schools. The use of the word "humanistic" here means that the school is concerned with the needs of people more than with the needs of the institution, a definition from which attention to self-concept and esteem naturally follows. We are not so naive as to ignore the current furor over humanism; those who use the term invite professional as well as personal attacks from the far right. In final anaylsis we do not care what such a climate is called so long as its characteristics are present and its effects on self-perceptions made possible. (Calling this type of climate "democratic" would be accurate and also fun: it would be amusing to hear our critics say that the schools should not be democratic.)

Our own research suggests an important example of humanistic climate applied to middle schools. We have asked transescents to tell us what things in school make them feel good about themselves. In doing so they have frequently made reference to a particular characteristic of teachers who enhance self-perceptions; namely, that those teachers are "nice." In the last fifteen years, professionals have been presented with many lists of characteristics of effective teachers. Oddly, this quality of "nice-ness" does not appear on those lists. Yet transescnets evidently feel that "nice-ness" is important and know it when they see it. We believe that professionals know what it means too. A nice teacher is one who knows students' names, knows something about them, is friendly, can give and take a joke, treats them with respect, and shows patience. A "not nice teacher" yells at students, humiliates them in front of peers, blames them when things go wrong, pushes them too hard, is secretive about what will be on the test, and assigns homework when there is a big social event scheduled. Nice teachers view transescents as human beings first and students second, while "mean" teachers have just the opposite view.

A third view of climate can be gleaned from the concept of the "invitational" school, one in which the attitudes and behaviors of the institution and adults invite transescents to find a place, to have dignity, and to learn (Purkey, 1978; Purkey and Strahan, 1986). Again research supports the idea that in this kind of school, learners seem to demonstrate more positive self-esteem and, not surprisingly, better academic achievement.

18

This is one of those cases where several independent research projects end up in the same place. Such corroboration should probably tell us something. When it comes to self-concept and esteem, climate counts and some climates are clearly better than others.

Decision-Making In School: Who Decides About Me?

The self-enhancing middle school helps transescents feel that their ideas are important and valuable. People who have positive self-esteem feel that they have some control over their lives wherever they happen to be. Often they find themselves in new situations where initially they feel powerless because they are in unfamiliar territory. As time goes by they begin to feel more competent if they find a place for themselves and gain some measure of personal control. This is internal locus of control. If events do not unfold this way they feel increasingly powerless and come to depend entirely on others to make decisions for them. This is external locus of control and it is usually accompanied by poor self-esteem and gradual alienation. So it is with transescents and their self-esteem in the middle school.

Unfortunately most school decisions are made by the adults in the institution. Transescents may find a place among a small clique of peers, but few have opportunities to have a say in the overall governance of the school or even day-to-day life in their classrooms. It is little wonder why some vandalize school property and consistently violate rules. After all, the school does not belong to them; it belongs to the adult gate-keepers of the institution.

Positive self-esteem means feeling one belongs, that he or she has a place. It also leads to self-direction and self-discipline. In order to pursue this possibility with transescents, middle school professionals must seek ways to involve them in decision-making in the school. Two ways of doing this are development of cooperative governance systems and use of teacher-student planning.

Having a cooperative governance system means that learners participate in formulation of policies, rules, regulations, and problem solutions. Some middle schools have student councils but these typically involve only a few students and the issues addressed are usually limited to planning social events. A few middle schools have gone beyond this and experimented with genuine participatory methods using a town meeting model. Done at the classroom, team, or schoolwide level this process involves open forums in which learners and adults come together to discuss, debate, and decide upon issues important to the group. Usually these are regularly scheduled meetings, chaired by students, with planned agendas. From hesitant beginnings, students gradually learn how to participate effectively and eventually come to act from a genuine perspective of being involved in running the school - which is exactly the point.

Another method for empowering learners is the use of teacher-student planning. In this case teachers involve individuals and groups of students in curriculum decision-making. Participation may range from selection of unit topics to deciding who will carry out which activities at what point in a unit. It may be done in any course or subject, even when plans are handed down from a state or district. This long-used technique is not the same as asking "what do you want to do today.'' Rather it is a systematic way of sharing power with learners so that they come to feel that their ideas and opinions are valued. Such feelings are a key ingredient in enhancing self-worth. This technique will be discussed more fully in Chapter 4.

These two methods are among many which may be used to help transescents gradually exercise more control over their lives in school. They reduce feelings of powerlessness and enhance self-esteem. They are worth trying.

Grouping: Where Do I Fit In?

The self-enhancing middle school provides opportunities for transescents to interact with peers of many types in an environment which accepts rather than avoids diversity. Learners are grouped on the basis of characteristics which school personnel believe learners possess. Those beliefs may or may not correspond with what learners believe about themselves. This placement in groups may confirm or raise doubts about aspects of the self-concept. In other words, grouping of students has the potential for affecting self-perceptions.

Many middle schools are engaged in a continuing debate over homogeneous versus heterogeneous grouping. Following the lead of the high school, most junior high schools used homogeneous grouping by ability and its near relative, tracking. As they became middle schools, many of these changed numerous practices, but kept away from proposals to alter grouping patterns. If they did raise the issue, verbal warfare usually broke out in faculty meetings and community sessions.

As it turns out, research findings on grouping have been accumulating for years. That research is older than the middle school movement and almost as old as junior high schools. The weight of its findings leans heavily in the direction of heterogeneous grouping. Specifically, research suggests that heterogeneous grouping is more favorable for academic achievement and, for our purposes here, affective development as well. As Findley and Bryan (1975) described it:

1. Homogeneous ability grouping as currently practiced shows no consistent positive value for helping students generally, or particular groups of students, to achieve more scholastically or to experience more effective learning conditions. Among the studies showing significant effects, the slight gain favoring high ability students is more than offset by evidence of unfavorable effects on the learning of students of average and below average ability, particularly the latter.

2. The findings regarding the impact on homogeneous ability grouping on affective development are essentially unfavorable. Whatever the practice does to build or inflate the esteem of children in the high ability groups is counterbalanced by evidence of unfavorable effects of stigmatizing those placed in average and below average ability groups as inferior and incapable of learning.

3. Homogeneous ability grouping, by design, is a separative educational policy, ostensibly according to students' test performance ability, but practically, according to students' socio-economic status and, to a lesser but observable degree, according to students' ethnic status.

20

Why then does the debate continue? And why do so many middle level schools use homogeneous grouping by ability? We believe the answer lies in the lens they use to view grouping possibilities. Put bluntly, students are grouped as a reflection of uninformed adult perceptions of teaching efficiency and learner self-esteem. Many teachers believe students will learn more in ability groups because it is easier to teach such groups.

This perception of ease or efficiency makes the teacher happy and he or she believes that this increased happiness will rub off onto the students. In most cases it doesn't work this way as these teachers forget that transescents have agendas different from their own. It is just too hard to remember that being with friends can be more important than being in an honors group or that learning is hindered when you are surrounded by low achievers and low teacher expectations to which you feel compelled to conform.

Picture a heterogeneous group of learners with diverse characteristics and a teacher with positive expectations for all. Imagine varied and interesting activities with students working in large groups, small groups, and independently. Picture peer tutoring, cooperative learning, varied materials, and lively discussions. Given those characteristics, imagine high achieving students modeling success, imagine those with histories of achievement problems getting caught up in the climate and flow of learning. This is a picture of a successful classroom for learners. If we deny the possibility of such portraits, we likewise deny the possibility of truly effective middle schools. The upshot, of course, is that this picture depends upon and builds from heterogeneous grouping.

Where does this portrait leave "gifted and talented" students on the one hand and mildly handicapped students on the other? It means that they are inappropriate in a middle school whose function is to provide quality general education for all students.

It should also be noted that research indicates that ability grouping and tracking may really be most clearly based on race and socio-economic status. Upper level groups are most often dominated by white, upper middle and higher class learners, while low tracks have a disproportionate number of minority and low socio-economic learners. Where this is the case, such tracking strips learners of their personal dignity. It also contributes to a class system in the schools. In the end, aside from academic and self-perception issues, ability tracking is undemocratic.

Grouping in a self-enhancing middle school begins with the assumption that transescents already have self-concept and esteem. In large measure they know what they can and can't do and also the strengths and weakness of others around them. They don't need the school to accentuate this knowledge base. Moreover their relationships (read "friendships" if you like) are not based on I.Q. or reading achievement. The social relationships of transescents are heterogeneous - thus heterogeneity is a natural starting point for school grouping. Teams or class groups might then function sometimes as a large group while at other times be broken down into smaller groups on the basis of interest, achievement, skill or talent, or the small groups might retain the heterogeneous characteristics of the larger group.

This kind of sub-grouping depends upon the objectives being pursued. At the same time groups ought to be fluid or dynamic in the sense that they change to fit the task. In this sense they recognize the multiple dimensions of the self-concept as well as the variability of learner skill and interest from one task to another. Thus responsible use of sub-grouping patterns for tutoring, cooperative learning, project activity, or direct teacher instruction does not violate the self-concept by introducing or suggesting dissonant ideas. It neither inflates nor debilitates self-perceptions. In the end, heterogeneous grouping followed by flexible sub-grouping is lifelike. For that reason it is a characteristic of the self-enhancing middle school.

Rules and Regulations, Rewards and Punishments: What Happens If I ...?

The self-enhancing middle school is one in which transescents may make the mistakes which are part of growing up without others giving up on them. Sometimes we act as if we don't trust learners, that if we don't tell them what they cannot do, they will surely do it. Perhaps this is why they are often greeted on the first day of school by long lists of rules and "thou shall not" speeches. The underlying message is "we don't trust you" and it is sad to even imagine that this would enter a student's concept: "People here don't trust me."

The process of growing up is the process of trying things out, of making mistakes and of finding success. Nowhere is this more visible in the attempts of transescents to figure out who they are and what they are capable of doing. On the other hand, a sense of competence and achievement is a basic emotional need of all people, including transescents, and without it negative self-esteem is almost guaranteed.

The system of rules and regulations as well as rewards and punishments used in a middle school ought to take these factors into account. We have already described possibilities for cooperative rule-making that help develop a sense of ownership among learners. The rules and regulations which result should be few in number and emphasize positive behaviors. The lengthier the list of rules, the more likely transescents are to forget some of them. And the fewer our attempts to describe, model, and teach desired behavior, the more likely some students will end up doing the wrong thing. The result is confusion, not only in the school, but in the minds of learners. Unfortunately, a confused person may also have difficulty finding ways to enhance his or her own self-esteem. Imagine a set of rules which says "here is what ought to happen and here is how to do it." The result is likely to be gradually more successful tries at doing the right thing and related boosts to self-esteem as they happen.

Such a system of rules and regulations emphasizes positive, pro-social behavior. In conjunction with it, the middle school should have an active program for recognizing and rewarding social development, as many do. These programs tend to follow a pattern of recognition followed by some special event or reward such as a luncheon with friends or a school shirt. This emphasis on positive behavior contributes to self-worth, a far cry from punishment systems that reinforce negative self-esteem. But what about those few learners who consistently violate school rules? Picture this: a principal invited to lunch several young people who were of this type. After eating, one of them finally asked, "Why am I here?" Having done some careful background work, the principal replied, "because you helped a sixth grader open his locker and I wanted you to know how much we appreciate that." Other members of this small group followed with the same question and each time the principal was able to name something that individual had done well.

Anti-social behavior does not pop up overnight. It gradually builds up over time and so does the anti-social self-concept that usually accompanies it. Here was a principal who realized this and took a first step to reverse the accumulating trend toward solidifying that self-description. Does this kind of action work? Yes, if it is done genuinely over a period of time as part of a system which emphasizes positive behavior and self-esteem. No, if it is a one-shot deal and the student is sent back into a system of negative feedback.

We were struck several years ago by a discipline program from Pulaski, Wisconsin which was explained by the following statement.

> We believe that a community's and a nation's greatest resource is its people, especially the students of our schools. At Pulaski Community Schools, the student is the nucleus of the school system and our educational decisions are guided by what we consider to be best for every student. We maintain that the student should be given every reasonable opportunity to realize his/her self.

> We are now, and should continue to be, a school offering students a second, third, and fourth chance. This means that every available alternative will be explored to help the student grow academically and in self-control. Each new opportunity in the area of discipline will be designed to encourage the students to accept responsibility for his/her actions. New alternatives in the area of academics will be explored, when necessary, to satisfy the student's needs and interests.

Again, the process of growing up is the process of trying things out; of making mistakes and finding successes. The middle school that realizes this fact and works with it turns discipline into a social process which supports the development of pro-social behavior and positive self-esteem.

Connecting With Parents: Is There Life Outside The School?

The self-enhancing middle school promotes constructive support for transescents in their lives outside the school. Those who study the stage called transescence make much ado about the emergence of the peer group, and rightly so. By their behavior and their statements transescents seem clearly on the move away from dependence on parents. However, it is a mistake to think that parents disappear from the sphere of influence. In reality peers become influential in most of day-to-day decisions such as dress, behavior, and group status while parents retain a role of significant other on bottom-line issues such as picking up the pieces after drug abuse, pregnancy, and trouble with the law. Peers may influence views of teachers, efforts in class, and attitudes toward school, but parents usually enter the picture when the grades go home.

Transescents have the best chance at positive mental health when both peers and parents are supportive. They are at risk when one or the other, or both, are lacking in support. For this reason it is important that middle school personnel encourage both peers and parents to act in constructive, enhancing ways.

The extent of parents' power is illustrated by an experimental study by Brookover (1965) with forty-nine ninth grade students who had achievement problems in school. For a period of nine months these students were divided into three groups. The first group worked with a counselor who played a positive and supportive role in evaluating the ongoing work of the group. The second group received continuous positive feedback from an outside "expert" (working with the study) about their work. The third group was given supportive feedback through their parents who, working with the researcher, developed improved expectations and feedback techniques for interacting with their children about school. The strength of parental influence was demonstrated by the finding that the first two groups had about the same level of improvement, while the third showed considerably more growth in their self-concepts as learners and in school achievement.

For middle level educators, the key question becomes, "How do we improve parental expectations and their feedback techniques?" For starters, it has become clear that many parents are simply unaware of the characteristics of transescence. They live with these young people and observe the symptoms of the stage yet are mystified by them. Like transescents, parents carry around a personal drama myth--only their version is, "this is only happening to my kid and me, not to others." Thus it is incumbent upon the school to use presentations, newsletters, group discussions, and other methods to share with parents the technical information about transescence which we usually reserve for faculty inservice sessions. For example, they ought to know about growth spurts, the declining age for achieving pubescence, the myths of the imaginary audience and personal drama, peer pressure, and the onset of formal operations. Once informed, their parental behavior may be more sensitive to the characteristics of transescents.

Middle schools should also provide opportunities for parents or guardians to learn techniques for interpersonal communications with transescents. Too often adults are unaware of the hidden curriculum in parent-child interactions. They need to know that the old saw, "you can do better if you try harder," is not always encouraging. They need to know that negotiation of limits is part of the autonomy - dependence struggle, not simply a sign of rebellion. They need to know the ways of saying, "I question your behavior," that do not also raise doubts about self-dignity.

Parents also need to hear from physicians, social workers, family counselors, law enforcement personnel, and other persons who have community contact with transescents. Through such school-sponsored opportunities, parents may come to know the services available to them when problems arise that are beyond their resolution skills.

Those who work in middle schools must continue their efforts to be sensitive to the shifting patterns in family types. Virtually all young people who experience changes in family organization, by divorce, separation, death or remarriage, must deal with self-concept change as well. A sense of loss or guilt may also contribute to loss of self-esteem. Such moments need not evolve into permanent problems with self-perception. However, school personnel must address such questions as,

"How do such young people feel if we describe the traditional, nuclear family as the most preferable unit?" "How do they feel when holidays are depicted as full-family occasions?" Is it realistic to expect young people to be fully on-task academically or to do all homework during times of family discontinuity?" In answering these questions, school personnel must again remember the transescent's personal agenda and its power to influence the school agenda.

Often we hear educators say that there is little they can do for the self-esteem of two or three young people because these few come from homes which are debilitating to their sense of self. It may well be true that there are some parents and guardians who are beyond our reach. However, the school is within our reach and it is important that for at least that period of time each day, these young people be treated with dignity and respect.

In the end, the effort to work with parents is not made simply to expedite the school's agenda. Instead it is aimed at creating and sustaining a home and community environment which supports the need for positive self-perceptions and overall mental health.

School Morale and Professional Self-Esteem: School Is Not Just For The Young

The self-enhancing middle school supports self-concept and esteem of adults as well as transescents. Youngsters aren't the only ones who come to school. So do teachers, administrators, counselors and other certified and non-certified adults. Just as the institution may have positive or negative effects on the self-esteem of learners, it can also affect that of the adults who work there. The middle school which is concerned with enhancing self-perceptions must attend to those of adults, as well as transescents, for two reasons. First, the adults in question are human beings and thus have a right to work in a place which supports self-worth. Second, we know that the self-perceptions of those adults, particularly teachers, seems to influence learners (Gilman, 1984).

Professional self-esteem emerges from the morale within the school, which in turn follows from the effects of institutional features. Where we find high morale, we are also likely to find positive self-esteem. Raths (1972) described eight emotional needs of children which also apply to adults. These include needs for achievement, belonging, self-respect, freedom from fear, freedom from guilt, economic security, love and affection, and self-concept and understanding. In analyzing the school for its possible effects on adult morale we might ask the following questions.

1. Do adults receive recognition for their accomplishments or do successes, large or small, go unnoticed?
2. Is this a place where adults feel they belong, or is conversation in the faculty room and other gathering areas likely to stop when one or another person walks in?
3. When adults look at themselves in the mirror do they like what they see or do they wonder why they are in education?
4. Can adults come to school without fearing for their physical or emotional health?

25

5. If something goes wrong, can adults chalk it up to experience, or do they have to fear sanctions from others?
6. Do adults have to worry about the next mortgage or rent payment, or can they do their work knowing such things are assured?
7. Is the school a playful place where adults exercise good humor, or is it a dull and lifeless place?
8. Are adults clear about their roles, rights and responsibilities, or are these things muddled and unclear?

One way to improve morale and thus enhance professional self-worth is to examine a particular middle school in light of questions like these. Surely all of us, from teachers to professors, have felt the sting of criticisms by the media and the public in recent years. But what counts in the end is the quality of one's everyday experiences which are embedded in the particular place we work. Hence work on morale in the middle school must focus on the individual building. With some success, a few have tried the following approach:

> A meeting was convened with the expressed purpose of working on adult morale and self-esteem in the school. After reviewing the list of emotional needs (previously cited), those present broke into small groups. Each group focused on one need and listed both positive and negative behaviors by teachers, administrators, other professionals, students, the school board, and the general public which impinged upon that need. The lists were then posted for all to read. New groups were then formed which would concentrate on each role group. Plans were made for informing each role group of the findings accompanied by ideas for building on the positives and putting a stop to the negatives.

The idea behind this kind of problem-solving workshop is that school morale and its influence on self-esteem can largely be controlled by the people within the school provided they are willing to work cooperatively toward that end. Furthermore, good morale will most likely be attained if the necessary attitudes and behaviors are clearly defined, publicly expressed, and mutually agreed upon.

Professional morale and self-esteem are currently in a tenuous position for several reasons. Recent years have seen an increase in public criticism, a trend toward centralized decision-making beyond local control, a loss in "real" dollar income for school people, and a move toward student achievement outcomes which are unrealistic for some learners and consequently frustrating for adults who work with them. The effects of these trends are seen in symtoms of negative self-esteem such as bitter attitudes, an exodus from the profession, and in-school withdrawal ("I just close my classroom door and work with my students"). Creating a collegial, in-school climate through activities like the workshop previously described, can certainly help morale and self-esteem. But it is also evident that several specific measures are necessary to insure continuing morale. These would include:

1. Decision-making processes which empower local professionals in areas like curriculum and governance.
2. Public recognition of professional achievement.

3. Improvements in conditions like class size, which influence student achievement that is a main source of professional self-esteem.
4. Clarification of student and professional expectations in ways that are realistic and attainable.
5. Improved arrangements for professional growth, staff development, and in-service education necessary for strengthening professional skills.
6. Use of procedures like peer coaching which encourage professionals to assume responsibility for their own improvement.
7. Sustained efforts to improve professional standing, including better economic conditions, within the profession.

We have focused here on improving self-concept and esteem as professionals. For adults who work in schools this is only one of many self-concept dimensions. Other dimensions emerge from their life outside the school and may, of course, influence what happens inside. It is customary to say that the school should only be concerned with out-of-school dimensions when they clearly interfere with in-school attitudes or behaviors. Unfortunately the message in that custom is this: we only care about one part of you, namely the part we use. Just as we are concerned with the larger life of young people, we should care about that of adults as well. Positive self-esteem and self-actualization are most possible when the greatest number of dimensions are perceived with satisfaction. Thus the self-enhancing school constructs opportunities for personal development such as employee assistance programs which contribute to overall mental health. At best, the blend of in-school efforts and out-of-school support creates an atmosphere in which adults view the institution as a constructive rather than debilitating force in their lives.

Summary

School as institution is an unavoidable metaphor. While institutional features can lead to unhappy conditions, they can also be arranged in self-enhancing ways through conscious decisions to do so. Among those are humanistic climate, cooperative governance, heterogeneous grouping, constructive rules and rewards, supportive connections with parents, and morale-enhancing activities.

Critics of these approaches sometimes say that such methods are manipulative. Of course, they are right. All education is manipulative. It attempts to improve or change the ways in which people perceive and behave. But there is a difference between manipulation which restricts perceptions and behaviors and that which liberates and empowers people. The institutional features of the self-enhancing middle school are designed for the latter purpose. They are intended to free transescents and middle school educators from practices which debilitate their self-dignity and self-esteem. Disregarding them makes for more than poor middle schools. It makes for inadequate environments for learning and growing. Anything less than an all out attempt to create a self-enhancing school is, in that sense, mis-educative.

Chapter 4
Self-Perceptions In School:
Curriculum and Teaching

The institutional features described in the last chapter are obviously powerful in the education of the transescents. What is learned from them is often more powerful than learnings from the planned, visible curriculum. But, in the self-enhancing middle school the overt plans for curriculum and teaching are also arranged in ways that promote clear self-concept and positive self-esteem.

Much of the talk about reform at the middle level begins with a description of transescent characteristics and then plunges into a myriad of structural innovations like block scheduling and team teaching. Certainly these organizational features support good programs, but the fact remains that *genuine change in schools only occurs as the nature of interactions between adults and learners changes.* Since these interactions are communicated through curriculum and teaching, those two topics must be at the core of thinking about effective middle schools. If they are not, then our plans for change are just so much talk.

In this chapter we consider two phases of planning to enhance self-perceptions. One has to do with ideas for various components in teaching-learning situations. The other is a brief description of some premium teaching procedures and programs.

CURRICULUM PLANNING IN THE
SELF-ENHANCING MIDDLE SCHOOL

Teaching-learning situations consist of six components: organizing centers, objectives, content, activities, materials, and measuring devices. In the best situations each of these components is carefully and thoughtfully planned with regard to both long and short-term experiences for learners. Where such curriculum planning is directed toward enhancing self-concept and esteem, those items are a part of the thinking at each step. In this section we will consider ideas related to self-perceptions which impinge upon each of the six components.

Organizing Centers

An organizing center is a broad topic, theme, problem, or issue around which the other components of curriculum plans revolve. It is the thread which runs through and unifies the experiences of learners. In classrooms where teaching and learning follow a textbook, the organizing centers are usually the various chapters in the particular text. Here, the influence on self-perceptions is indirect as far as curriculum planning is concerned though it may be powerful, especially on school or subject related self-images. Depending upon climate, grouping, achievement, teacher behavior, and other factors, transescents may come to feel good or bad about themselves with regard to school self-concept.

However, when one aims to enhance self-concept and esteem, curriculum planning must also consider organizing centers which are drawn from the real needs and interests of transescents and which may thus more directly affect self-perceptions. Here arrangements are made in the school program to plan and implement units on such topics as "getting along with others," "living in school," "how transescents fit in the community," "understanding the messages in commercial media." In each case the organizing center reflects a concept embedded in the real lives of learners. Figure 4.1 illustrates an array of sources from which such organizing centers might be drawn. Again, the sources are items which influence self-perceptions of learners.

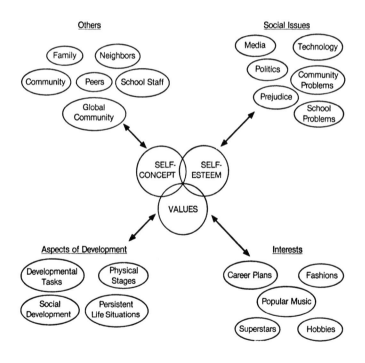

Figure 4.1

Sources of Organizing Centers

From Beane, J. and Lipka, R. *Self-concept, self-esteem and the curriculum.* New York: Teachers College Press, 1986.

29

From a historical perspective the selection of organizing centers which reflect transescent needs and interests is a long standing idea. As early as the 1920's, advocates of this approach developed the "project" method which was a forerunner of the more modern experience-based unit approach. In the 1940's and 50's many junior high schools organized core programs which were supposed to use the needs approach taught by a single teacher in a block-time program (Lounsbury and Vars, 1978). This concept will be discussed later under premium curriculum arrangements. Most recently the approach has been described in terms of the spontaneous organization of units around questions or issues which teachers perceive to be of current concern among learners (Stevenson, 1986).

Whatever the name or whatever the organization the real issue here is whether middle school educators are sufficiently concerned with self-perceptions to devote time to units directly addressing self-concept and esteem. Granted the institutional features of the school may be arranged so as to enhance self-perceptions regardless of curriculum content. However, the truly self-enhancing middle school eventually must attempt a more direct approach through interest - and needs - based organizing centers. And, to the extent that such topics more clearly represent the common needs of all learners than do academic subject areas, one might wonder whether the former should eventually comprise the general education requirements of the middle school instead of the present collection of academic subjects.

Objectives

The self-enhancing middle school is explicitly concerned with development of self-concept and esteem. Teaching-learning situations are most likely to enhance self-perceptions if the objectives which guide them include explicit statements for that purpose. Too often our objectives are limited to academic content or skills as if personal development is simply a side issue which will happen by chance. Worse yet, there are still some educators who believe that self-concept in transescents is a function of academic achievement alone.

When we develop or review statements of objectives, we ought to look for balance among them in terms of affective, cognitive, psychomotor, and academic examples. It is the affective objectives that introduce the personal element into a unit, encouraging learners to find personal meanings and integrate learnings into their self-perceptions. If the unit being studied focuses on some social problem or emerging need of transescents, such objectives are easily developed. If the unit is embedded in a more abstract subject area thought must be given to how the topic might relate to the on-going lives of learners through application of skills and content to real life situations. For example, objectives in general mathematics should consider how computational skills could be used in unit buying, buying on time payment plans, keeping records for clubs, saving for special events or managing jobs like babysitting or newspaper routes.

Objectives must also be stated in ways that allow for personal interpretation. Those that specify a single way of doing something or demonstrating achievement ignore the diverse ways in which individual learners might approach objectives and thus obstruct the self-esteem of any who may vary from the prescribed way. One interesting proposal for developing objectives is to include some which Eisner

(1969) calls "expressive." For example, instead of saying "To identify ten types of birds found at the zoo," the objective might say, "to visit the zoo and discuss what we saw there." The latter statement provides opportunities for learners to exercise personal interests and perceptions and to find personal meanings. Hence, everyone may find success at the zoo, not just those who can see what the teacher wants them to see.

Finally, in actually carrying out a unit the statement of objectives should be made available to the learners. When purposes of learning are hidden from learners they are likely to be unsure or confused about what they are supposed to accomplish. As noted before, when a person is in a confusing or uncertain situation, their self-perceptions are at risk. Better that learners should know where they are going so they may proceed with confidence and self-assurance.

Content

The self-enhancing middle school encourages transescents to see personal meaning in the ideas around them. Some people are confused about the role of content in curriculum plans. They think the content is the objective, that mastery of information is the aim of education. Actually content is comprised of the important facts, principles, and concepts which help learners pursue objectives related to affective, psychomotor and cognitive growth. Content is only meaningful and valuable insofar as it genuinely does make such contributions. Thus when we consider the relation between the content of curriculum plans and transescent self-perceptions, we ask to what extent that content broadens self-understanding and strengthens self-esteem.

As it turns out, the further removed content is from the personal issues of transescent life, the less likely it is to be learned and used. Unfortunately, many teachers are forced to teach content which is remote from learners' lives and they struggle to find ways to make it meaningful for learners. It is not that these people don't care about self-perceptions; it is that they feel powerless to "change the curriculum." However, most content can be brought to life if teachers are willing to be creative in how they use it.

First, virtually all content may be taught at three levels: fact, concept, and value (Harmin, et al., 1973). Suppose, for example, we begin with the skill of calculating unit costs. By using word problems, we may introduce the concept of unit pricing in grocery shopping. Then by wording of the problems and through discussions we might ask students to consider whether the economic savings in some unit pricing outweigh the environmental costs (e.g. bottles vs. cans). In this case we have related standard mathematics content to questions of values in real life.

Content can also be brought to life by reconsidering traditional notions of sequencing. Many people believe that content must be mastered before interesting and/or affective issues are raised. Not only is this concept untrue, but its application to learning situations inhibits the chance for learners to perceive worth in content.

Suppose, for example, that we want learners to know about events in the American Revolutionary War. In one scenario, we might have them memorize important events, dates, and persons. In another scenario we might begin by discussing conflict between transescents and their parents regarding curfews, peer

31

relations, or other typical situations. In doing so, the learners may be helped to see that in these conflicts, they feel mistreated or powerless, become frustrated and, subsequently, verbally aggressive. They want, instead, to have a role in decision-making, to be heard and understood. This case may then be used to introduce the concept of revolution, as a large scale, national version of the frustration-aggression cycle. Finally, as a specific case we may use the cycle to show learners the causes of the American revolution, and other revolutions as well. Unlike the first scenario, the second opens up the possibility for finding personal meaning, for improving understanding, and for relating the present to the "remote" past. By proceeding back through the fact, concept, value levels we may also raise questions which help learners clarify personal beliefs about current events. Here we have brought the content to life by introducing personal feelings and perceptions. While we have violated the traditional concept of "facts first, issues later," the chances for learning have been increased. It is this kind of process which Dewey (1902) referred to as "psychologizing" subject matter. It means that the content is related to the life of the learner.

Content may also be brought to life through the use of certain kinds of activities which we will discuss in succeeding sections. Before leaving this one, however, a word is necessary about how affective content is perceived. Often critics of affective approaches say that such methods have no content. Such an accusation is without merit. Of course there is content. It just happens to be different from traditional academic content. The perceptions of learners are content and so are the ideas which permeate the issues in their lives. The facts about drugs represent content and so do the concepts presented in commercial media which impact on transescent lives. As to their rigor, these types of content are at least as difficult to work with as those from traditional subject areas. Perhaps the real problem for the critics is that such content is more interesting to learners. Or maybe such subject matter hasn't gathered any dust on it. It is fresh and alive, and it has the potential for promoting essential personal-social growth of transescents.

Activities

The self-enhancing school provides opportunities to engage in personally significant experiences. For transescents, self-perceptions emerge largely from the activities in which they engage and the ways in which they perceive the outcomes of those activities (Lipka and Brinthaupt, 1987). Each time they try to do something they are using some dimension of their self-concept: "I am a person who does this or that." As a result of each activity they receive feedback from others or engage in self-reflection about what happened. This intrinsic or extrinsic feedback may strengthen, debilitate, validate, or confuse their self-esteem. In other words, activities provide opportunities to try out the self-concept and test the self-esteem. For this reason, the day-to-day learning activities of the curriculum are a crucial part of enhancing self-perceptions in the middle school.

In our research we found that when transescents talked about what made them feel good about themselves in school, they often referred to the nature of learning activities: "fun." By that they did not mean purely whimsical, non-directed activities. Rather, they referred to what might technically be called "active, hands-on learning activities," those which involve doing something rather than mere passive listening or test-taking. "Fun" activities may include simple exercises, small projects, and the like. They may also function on a larger scale. Picture this:

A group of sixth grade students and teachers undertook a unit on Ancient Egypt. As part of the unit they constructed the interior of an Egyptian Tomb. One classroom was set aside and a smaller room within that one was built using wood and construction paper. Inside this "tomb" five alcoves were constructed, each one for a particular pharoah. For example, in King Tut's alcove was a platform on which was placed a decorated sarcophagus and mummy. Behind the platform was a shelf holding canopic jars fashioned from paper mache. The paper walls were decorated with hieroglyphics. A secret passage led to another room in which were displayed salt map models of the Nile River Valley, costumes, pictures, charts, early machines, and term papers on Egyptian topics. Other students and parents were invited to visit the tomb and experience ancient foods and entertainment.

This is an example of a grand-scale version of what transescents call "fun" activities. It is much different from simply reading about Ancient Egypt and answering the questions at the end of the chapter. Here was a chance to not only learn a lot about a topic but to take away from the unit something personal. Every student could point with pride and a sense of achievement to the part of the tomb and related projects that he/she had built, made, or written. And we can guess with considerable certainty that the feedback from parents and other students contributed immensely to the participants' self-esteem.

Activities which enhance self-esteem are "fun," and also interactive. Imagine the small group constructing the tomb interacting, making decisions, shifting roles as leader and follower as various kinds of skill were required. Imagine the sense of responsibility needed to carry out the project and the sense of accomplishment at its completion. We offer this activity partly as an example of these various dimensions of self-enhancing activities. We also use it here to show that this kind of activity can bring even a topic as dead as Ancient Egypt to life. Imagine what might happen if the topic itself were contemporary.

Resources

The self-enhancing middle school exposes transescents to a variety of possibilities for looking at themselves. Like other aspects of the curriculum, the learning resources we use have the potential for influencing transescent self-perceptions. Many of the resources used in schools probably have little to do with self-images since they are simply descriptions of events or ideas. However, others contain much by way of self-concept and esteem messages, while still others are devoted entirely to that purpose.

Much has been said about race, age, and sex bias in materials and from the view of self-perceptions even more of the same is needed. The portrayal of minorities in educational materials has been a sad chapter in our profession. Granted, considerable progress toward breaking stereotyped images has been made in this area, but there are evidently some who still feel that biased images are not harmful and, worse yet, some who believe they are reasonable and perhaps desirable. One area which requires new attention is the way in which transescents themselves are portrayed. Too often young people are seen in passive, submissive, roles "doing what kids are expected to do." Much less often do we see transescents reading or viewing materials which cast them in creative, responsible, decision-making roles. One can only wonder what message learners take away from these materials.

Another problem with text oriented resources is that their over-emphasized use puts transescents in situations where they must learn what someone else thinks is important about a topic and then answer questions reflecting the author's interest. Thus learners have little opportunity to find their own personal meanings and explore their own interests on a topic. Remember, middle school is the level where we begin to ask, "What do you think the author had in mind when she wrote this story?" leaving little time to ask, "How did this story make you feel?" Used this way educational materials, especially textbooks, contribute to feelings of personal powerlessness and apathy.

For those in search of resources which address self-perceptions, the market is bountiful. Books, videos, computer simulations and other materials developed to encourage self-thinking are widely available. In addition, every community is filled with people who can interact with learners and every school contains peers and adults who can serve as resources. The key here is that resources, including people and materials, that might enhance self-perceptions are the kind which promote interaction. These resources lead transescents to think about themselves, to ask questions, to learn about their lives, and to expand their views of their futures.

Regretably such resources have fallen on hard times as their use is criticized by those who would prefer that transescents not think about themselves or question the world around them. No matter how it is said, these people want youth to do and believe what they are told to do and believe. It is sad that such adults would want to limit the creativity, thinking, and decision-making of transescents at precisely the stage where their development begins to allow for serious insight, beginning independence, thoughtful consideration of alternatives, and the search for values. And how depressing it is to hear of so many cases where schools are afraid to use affective and cognitive (thinking) resources for fear of criticism. While many educators have been able to stand firm for enhancing personal-social growth, others have been beaten down by real or perceived threats. As we write this, the courts are considering the question of whether young people will have the chance to see diversity or be limited to the views of one or another public pressure group, and whether opinion alone will be accorded the same status as ideas based on thoughtful evidence. Perhaps the right of young people to think and learn will win out. Perhaps not. Perhaps the resources and programs we use will be declared as unconstitutional intrusions and thus illegal for "public" schools. For any who think this possibility is overstated, they should remember that in some testimony before Congress, the list of "secular humanist" practices has included "middle schools."

Evaluation Devices

The self-enhancing middle school helps transescents learn how to evaluate themselves. Since self-esteem is largely influenced by feedback from what we do, evaluation devices play a crucial role in enhancing self-perceptions. The most powerful feedback is that which comes from significant others, pertains to matters of personal importance, and is communicated in personally meaningful ways. Evaluation devices with these three characteristics are most powerful.

Significant others are chosen by the individual and may selectively include family members, peers, school officials, or anyone else. The individual may also selectively exclude any one of those groups or individuals within them. Whatever the reasons for either action, and they may be many, significant others are chosen by the individual and cannot be forced upon him or her. To see this theory in action, one need only notice how learners react strongly or indifferently to feedback from different people. For transescents, parents/guardians and peers are most often chosen as significant others while teachers hold less sway. Also, the choice of one group or person over another may change with time and circumstances. In light of this, teachers must look for ways to be certain that parents and peers encourage and compliment progress toward school goals. They must also strive for ways to emphasize the positive in transescents' efforts, since those individuals who give constantly negative feedback are likely to lose what significance they might have.

Teachers and other school officials must stare long and hard at the kinds of evaluation and feedback processes they use to be certain that they are carried out in ways which are personally meaningful for transescents. In doing so, they must clearly recognize the fact that if learners do not care about school tasks, they probably will not care about their evaluation either. Where curriculum plans are brought to life through projects, cooperative learning, and connections to transescent lives, evaluation and feedback are most likely to be taken seriously and even sought out. Given these conditions, what are some ways of making evaluation self-enhancing?

Imagine a transescent learner awaiting the return of some test, homework assignment, or essay. Taking the paper in hand, he glances quickly at the top (which for many learners is also the "bottom line"). There in bold red is "-5." Or, perhaps, a scan of two pages of writing reveals a mass of teacher remarks in bold red ink each one noting a mistake. What is the message here? In the first case it is "you were wrong five times," and in the second, "this paper is full of errors." In both instances the emphasis is on the negative and the message is, "we are most aware of what you cannot do." Over time, the metaphor is clear: this school operates on a deficit model where what is important is finding weaknesses and pointing them out. Imagine instead that the first paper is marked "+95" or that the essay reactions note several things that were done well in addition to pointing out a few problems. Here the messages are quite different: this work has many good things about it even though there are also mistakes. Simple as these examples are, they illustrate powerful messages about self-esteem, especially if the days or years of learner's school experiences are full of one or the other type.

35

If we want young people to feel competent and adequate about themselves, then we must systematically point out those things that they do well. This rule applies not only to written exercises, problems, or tests, but to verbal feedback as well and also to group work, question responses, physical activities, and projects. To be truly self-enhancing, such a climate must pervade the school. At the same time, adults must remember that individual success should not always be a public matter. Some transescents prefer not to be publicly recognized because they fear they will be singled out or even rejected by peers. Others don't mind attention and a few might even relish it. Before any public recognition is given, the individual should be given a choice in the matter. These are transescents with their imaginary audience and they should have the right to go on stage or not whether for sports, social behavior, and yes, the honor roll too.

Efforts to shift emphasis from negative to positive feedback must also be extended to peers and parents. Since such behavior is learned, the school program needs to include attempts to teach both groups about the power and skills of constructive feedback. In the case of peers such learnings may be a part of specially designed units contained in regular classes or in advisory groups. In the case of parents the task is more complicated but certainly possible. The idea of emphasizing positive accomplishments should show up in newsletters, on "back-to-school" night, at meetings of parent teacher associations, and in sessions on parenting skills. It should also be modeled in the more occasional contacts school people have with parents. Imagine how discouraging it must be for parents to meet with teams and listen to four or five teachers go on for almost an hour about all the things their son or daughter is doing wrong. Even where the problems are many, there are always genuine examples of strength or accomplishment for any learner. These must be clearly and explicitly described along with areas that need improvement. Otherwise the parents are likely to doubt themselves as well as their child and to leave feeling hopeless, confused, or as is often the case, disgusted. Enhancement of self-perceptions in the home can hardly be expected to grow out of such beginnings. And what about those parents who simply do not come to school? Is it that they don't care, as we often say, or could it be that all they ever hear from the school is bad news about their child? Who wants to hear that again anyway?

In this same vein, educators must also stare at "report cards" which are sent home. Here the middle school might well draw from the example of primary schools. At the earlier level, report cards typically include lists of skills and behaviors which have been on the agenda and notations are made of which ones have been accomplished and which need more work. They also include anecdotal statements from the teacher and often these comments are purposely aimed at the positive. This is a far cry from the single letter grades or numbers and impersonal computer-programmed comments which make up so many of our middle school report cards. Sure the primary teachers have fewer students. Some middle schools have advisory teachers do the written parts while others do so by dividing students among team members. Whatever the procedure, the time is worth it because the message is important. Simple letter grades and computer statements do little to enhance self-perceptions in serious ways. Personal messages do much more.

Perhaps the most powerful way to connect evaluation devices to self-perceptions is through the use of self-evaluation by learners. The skills of self-evaluation are learned and thus must be taught. Since most transescents cannot be expected to have had previous experience with self-evaluation, we might begin on a small scale by having them hand in work with their own evaluation of it attached. This might be done through a checklist or by reacting to guiding questions from the teacher.

Eventually the time should come when reports to the home include self-evaluative material from learners. For example, checklists of work habits or social behavior might have columns for both student and teacher reactions. Students may fill out sentence completion forms on a variety of school related topics. Or, learners might write a few paragraphs about their work using specific questions about what was to be accomplished, what was actually done, what problems were encountered, what needs improvement, and so on. Some teachers who use this last method also ask students to keep weekly logs that are used to recall material for the larger evaluation. In any of these types, teachers may review the self-evaluations and note agreement or disagreement and, in the case of the latter, confer with the student and/or parents. This use of self-evaluation does more than simply develop evaluation skills. It helps transescents feel that they have an important role to play in assessing their own work. It helps them to assume responsibility. It promotes accurate and realistic self-concept. And, it brings personal meaning to the evaluation process.

These, then, are some of the ways in which middle school evaluation devices might be used to enhance self-perceptions. When moving in this direction educators must constantly remember that positive self-esteem is the most powerful motivator in achievement, both socially and academically. No matter what some people say, failure rarely breeds success. Learning may involve mistakes and it may be a struggle. But, in the end, success leads to success. In designing evaluation devices for middle school learners, the emphasis must be on those things done well and their recognition must come from the individual as well as peers, parents, and teachers.

PREMIUM PROGRAMS AND PROCEDURES

All this talk about needed work on institutional features and curriculum planning does not mean that middle schools have no standing examples of self-enhancing arrangements. Just as concern for personal-social growth has been a longstanding concern at the middle level, so have programs and procedures to address that concern. In the next few pages we will describe a few of these that have a wide reputation, recognizing at the same time that individual teachers and local schools could fill several volumes from their own experience.

Cooperative Learning

The self-enhancing middle school encourages transescents to learn how to work well with others. Transescents have a powerful drive to form relationships with peers, to find a place in the group, and to earn some degree of status. This drive is so powerful that individuals will risk conflict with adults and give up some aspects (e.g. dress, language) of their individuality for it. Yet when one looks at most middle schools there seems to be an overriding rule: Thou shalt not interact with peers. In classrooms side conversations are hushed, furtive notes intercepted and thrown away, and directions given not to work with "your neighbor." At a time when peer relationships are most desired, the tide of the school flows against them. This crucial part of transescents self-perceptions is to be carried out before or after school, between classes, or in the cafeteria. And, just when the possibility for learning cooperation is most acute, the school attempts to heat up the competition using competitive reward structures and normative grading systems.

In the past few years a growing body of research has demonstrated that a powerful method called cooperative learning can successfully reverse this odd inclination of the school to contradict the natural tendencies of transescence. Evidence suggests that cooperative reward structures can promote positive self-esteem while also enhancing academic achievement (Slavin, 1981; Johnson, Johnson, Holubec and Roy, 1984). In other words, it is an arrangement which ought to pervade the middle school.

Cooperative learning may take many forms. One is peer tutoring, long known to have a significant impact on learning for both the tutor and the tutee. Its other forms are actually grander versions of peer tutoring, building as they do on the idea that kids learn best from people they like, understand, and relate to - namely peers. Slavin (1981) describes several kinds of cooperative learning arrangements ranging from team tournaments to small group completion of a single worksheet to open-ended group investigation of a particular topic. Another, which we will use for illustration here, is called the "jigsaw" method. Suppose a teacher divides a unit into five sub-topics. Small groups are formed to study each topic and, with teacher help, to become "experts" on the topic. After a week or two new groups are formed, each one consisting of one representative from each expert group. Within this interdisciplinary group, individuals teach the others about their sub-topic and the group develops a project bringing together all of the sub-topics.

In such an arrangement there is the excitement and appeal of peer interaction. There is the possibility for academic gain in the idea of learning from peers. And, there is the chance for each individual to earn status in the group since the group needs what each member knows or can do. It is in this last advantage that we find the probable reason for increased self-esteem demonstrated in research and practice. Each member of the group, no matter what that individual's previous status, has an important place. As work on a project goes on, other skills such a leadership may emerge, but the project falls short if any individual's contribution is left out.

Some teachers are reluctant to try this technique. They think this is the old "what do you want to do today" technique. Far from it, this is structured small group work with evidence of success behind it. Or, they fear that one or another individual will not pull his or her weight and the rest of the group will complain. Rather than being a disadvantage, this is actually a real chance for learning. How else but through direct experience can we help young people learn about the problems of group work and how to deal with them. Among those who are reluctant, a few feel cooperative learning is too time-consuming and too much bother. We can only wonder what those complaints have to do with the effort to provide quality learning.

Finally, there are those who feel that the school should emphasize competition, muttering something about "real life" and "that dog-eat-dog world out there." This is sad logic to use on transescents who are not adults, who do not choose to be in school, who yearn for peer interaction, and whose learning of cooperative skills and attitudes could bring us closer to the democratic ideal.

Community Service Projects

One of the needs of transescents is that of achieving a sense of competence and self-worth. At the same time, one of the characteristics of those at this stage is an emerging sense of altruism, a desire to help others. Put together, these two aspects of transescence suggest the possibility of helping these young people to feel adequate by involving them in projects of service to others.

One of the best ways of doing this is through school-sponsored community service programs (Lipka, Beane, and O'Connell, 1985). Under the auspices of the school, such a program takes transescents out of the school into the community where they may help elders, assist in day care centers, conduct community surveys, work to improve community recreation programs, help with environmental problems, and so on.

Over the years, community service programs have been found much more frequently at the high school level than at the middle level. However, recent experience in many middle schools has shown that transescents are quite capable of responsibly participating in this type of experience. In fact, it has often been said that if one needs volunteers to help with a service project, one of the best groups to turn to is middle schoolers, who are characteristically seeking chances for commitment and affirmation. We do recommend that if such programs are undertaken at the middle level, that participation be based on group rather than individual projects. This suggestion evolves from the transescents' search for peer connections and the fact that many may not have had previous experience with service projects. Also, it is important to remember that transescents are characterized as having evolving and shifting interests. Consuming commitment to collecting canned goods today may tomorrow be directed at a "Save the Buffalo" campaign. Service projects should have clear goals, a relatively short implementation period, and sponsors who understand the vagaries of transescent altruism.

These caveats aside, research has demonstrated a positive connection between participation service projects and learner self-esteem (Hedin and Conrad, 1980; Newmann and Rutter, 1983). Clearly such projects provide opportunities for transescents to develop self-worth and to earn a place in the community. At a time when adults are so likely to think poorly of youth, experience has also shown that service projects enlighten citizens about the competence of transescents and their capacity to care about others.

Adviser-Advisee Programs

Earlier we suggested that paying attention to self-concept and esteem is part of the historical notion of the middle level school as a guidance school. Unfortunately, when many people think of guidance they think only of guidance departments and professionally certified counselors. Instead, middle school advocates need to envision guidance opportunities pervading the whole program or as the slogan proposes, "guidance everyday for every student." The support that transescents need (for personal-social growth) is simply too much for counselors in traditional guidance organization to undertake (Alessi and Toepfer, 1971). They are too few in number and too burdened with course/content problems, quasi-administrative tasks, and the few "difficult" cases.

To address these shortcomings many middle schools have developed advisor-advisee programs (a.k.a. "advisory", "teacher advisory", "home-based" programs). Organized as separate programs (James, 1986) or included within class "core" type organization (Vars, 1987), advisory programs are designed to deal directly with the affective needs of transescents. Activities may range from non-formal interactions to use of systematically developed units whose organizing centers are drawn from the common problems, needs, interests, or concerns of transescents, such as "Getting Along with Peers," "Living in the School," or "Developing Self-Concept." In the best of these programs, transescents have an opportunity to get to know one school adult really well, to find a point of security in the institution, and to learn about what it means to be a healthy human being.

Middle level professionals who advocate these programs understand one of the odd ironies in schooling: we want young people to read, so we teach them directly to read; we want young people to write, so we teach them directly to write; we want young people to have positive mental health, but we expect that it will emanate out of some indirect part of the school program. To top things off, we are then surprised when it doesn't. The fact is that if you really want someone to learn something, you have to "teach" it to him/her. With regard to affective education in general and self-concept/esteem in particular, this is just what advisory programs are meant to do.

Block-Time Core Programs: Single Teacher or More

When asked to explain why elementary school teachers seem better able than high school teachers to organize interdisciplinary units, use flexible time, get to know students, and demonstrate patience and sensitivity, those in the higher grades often use a standard reply: "If I had a self-contained classroom with a smaller class size, I could do those things too." The advantages of the self-contained classroom are so widely recognized that it is a wonder that middle school educators, especially those concerned with learner-centered approaches, have not more actively tried to adapt that organization to their level.

In reality a precedent for this kind of organization at the middle level has already been developed. In the 1940's and 50's many junior high schools organized single teacher, block-time programs under such titles as "core", "unified studies", and "common learnings" (Vars, 1987). In these programs a single teacher was scheduled to work in two or three period blocks with a single group of learners. The teacher was usually responsible for language arts and social studies as well as guidance. While the actual curriculum emphasis varied in practice, these core programs were intended to promote use of units organized around interdisciplinary, social problems, and youth needs approaches. Furthermore, the core program represented the required common learnings program of all students while other portions of the day were given over to specialized subject areas. Fanaticism over separate subject academic learnings, not unlike that of the 1980's, led to dismantling of core programs following the launching of Sputnik in 1957. Today this arrangement is rarely found in middle level schools though it still survives, and thrives, in a few places.

For the middle school concerned with enhancing self-perceptions, single-teacher core programs offer several advantages. First, this adaptation of the self-contained classroom offers an excellent transition arrangement from the elementary school to the subject-centered, departmentalized high school. Second, the teacher may get to know the group well and thus develop greater sensitivity to individual needs, interests, problems and concerns. Third, flexibility with the block of time may allow for greater use of techniques such as teacher-student cooperative planning, group work, and development of projects. Fourth, the interdisciplinary basis of the program encourages the use of problems and needs approaches to curriculum organization. Finally, the learners have more opportunities to get to know one another and the teacher through extended interaction.

Obviously, the development of interdisciplinary teams was partly an attempt to replicate the single-teacher core program in light of certification regulations based on single subjects and the desire to retain academic specialization. To some extent interdisciplinary teaming has encouraged sensitivity to learners through team planning as well as the use of interdisciplinary curriculum units. However, this arrangement has met with mixed results because of reluctance by some team members to embrace the concept, scheduling difficulties, and the limited understanding of higher levels of interdisciplinary curriculum through problems and needs approaches.

As the middle school movement continues to evolve the single-teacher core approach should receive renewed attention, particularly at the sixth grade. Given its potential advantages with regard to enhancing self-perceptions it certainly deserves a second look.

Teacher-Student Planning

Teacher-student planning means teachers and students working in a partnership to articulate a problem/concern, develop objectives, locate resources and evaluate progress in fulfilling objectives.

Teacher-student planning is seen as the ultimate expression of school as a democratic institution—an institution built upon shared leadership and a democratically conceived policymaking program. Within such an institution, personal-social growth and learning the techniques of democratic action are given greater emphasis than the learning of fixed amounts or types of subject matter. Krug (1950) indicates that schools with this orientation will be characterized by group (administrators, teachers, pupils) effort and cooperative planning seriously addressing the issues of "Why?", "What?", "When?", "Who?", "How?", and "Where?".

Making the transition from teacher-exclusive to teacher-student planning is not a "sink or swim" proposition. Rather it should be a developmental process involving increasing amounts and complexity with increasing time. Teachers wishing to make a commitment to this planning technique should undertake the following steps.

1. Make the first step a small and concrete one. Perhaps start with a determination of role and functions of room jobs and committees, e.g., plant waterer, lunch counter, bulletin board committee, etc.

2. Movement into academic areas should be undertaken by planning for short periods of time with a focus upon something that has a high probability of success, as nothing breeds success like success. Perhaps the planning of an around-the-school-grounds nature walk for the concept of "change" in science; or a "no bake" cookie manufacturing experience to apply the principles of manufacturing and marketing.

3. Involve another teacher or two in the process. Teaching can be a lonely profession in terms of day-to-day contact with fellow teachers. Attempting something new can benefit from the mutual support of individuals planning together, talking about what they hope to accomplish, and how they plan to accomplish it. In reality, planning with another teacher or two helps to refine and reinforce those very planning skills that are needed in working with students.

It should come as no surprise that the elements of teacher-student planning are the same elements we consider in any sort of planning for effective instruction. The difference resides in the degree of involvement for students within the process. In defining the problem and/or setting the goals, the focal point of the element is addressing the question: *"What should be studied?"* The answer may be an outgrowth of an exploratory experience that was introduced by the teacher or a pupil in the class. More than likely it will be an outgrowth of a social problem or student need for which a serious effort is made to poll all students and build consensus. To facilitate the process, the initial efforts in teacher-pupil planning should be addressed to establishing a set of criteria that can be used as a guide for the selecting of future problems of study. In preparation for such a criteria-setting discussion you should consider questions such as those articulated by Anderson (1956):

1. **Are the proposed goals appropriate to the maturity of the group and do they build upon previous experiences?**

An early and important task of the teacher is to ascertain the entering behavior of these students. That is, what are the students bringing to the situation in terms of prior knowledge, skills, and attitudes. The task of interviewing the chief of police concerning local pre-teen and teen drug abuse will take on two distinct instructional forms based upon the presence or absence of interviewing skills and/or a knowledge base of drug abuse in young people.

2. **Will the goals give each pupil a chance to succeed and to use his own talent and interests in contributing to the group?**

In some respects this is the logical extension of the first question in that it requires even further knowledge of the entering behaviors of the students. Each student needs to have a chance to be successful and gain the feelings and attitudes that come from being successful. To ensure this we need to encourage goals that will allow for the utilization of students' avocations and talents.

3. **Are the goals varied enough to provide for balanced development in the cognitive, affective, and psychomotor domains?**

In planning with students we need to ensure experiences that will provide the growth of students intellectually, physically, emotionally, and socially. Goals that lend themselves to research, writing, group discussions, building models, role playing, playing games, and observing should be encouraged. At any one point in time student interests/needs may lead to an imbalance in the learning domains. This imbalance should be noted and addressed in teacher-student planning that takes place later in the school year.

4. **Are the goals recognized by the students as a means for achieving their purposes?**

Ascribing personal meaning to the goals provides students with a purpose for learning. More permanent learning takes place in an environment of self-direction and personal ownership of the learning agenda.

5. **Do the goals provide opportunities for the students to work cooperatively in selecting, planning, carrying out, and evaluating specific instructional activities?**

Compelling evidence is mounting from the cooperative learning research effort (e.g. Johnson, Johnson, Holubec and Roy, 1984). The opportunity to work and plan together improves student self-esteem, promotes academic achievement, fluid friendship circles, and positive attitudes towards students in general and teachers in particular.

6. **Will the goals broaden the students' interests and concerns?**

As discussed on numerous occasions by Fraenkel (1980) schools afford students the opportunity to expand and improve their esthetic, practical, and moral judgments. The goals selected should help students decide if certain things are better than other things, as well as being honestly receptive to the reasons other individuals offer for judging things as "better" or "best."

7. **Are the goals such that the materials, resources, and equipment needed are available or can be constructed by the students?**

Nothing grinds the teacher-student planning process to a halt quicker than agreeing upon activities for which the materials are unavailable. However, do not overlook the resourcefulness of your students in designing/building needed materials. One of the authors still recalls with amazement the ability of his sixth graders to construct mazes, gerbil cages, incubators, and other equipment necessary to deal with the "other animal forms" phase of a unit in human growth and development.

8. **Do the goals make it possible to use the students' community as a laboratory for learning?**

There is a real need to plan activities that place persons, places, and things on an equal footing with print resources. Learning is more apt to be viewed as meaningful when it takes place in a real live community setting.

In formulating/writing specific learning outcomes, two related activities might be used. Students can dictate their ideas to the teacher in an experience chart format with later refinement into objectives if necessary. Or, students could be taught a straight-forward procedure for writing objectives. A discussion of action verbs as "words that describe what you are doing" within a sentence that tells you "what you are going to work on" can be very successful as an objectives writing activity. A third possibility especially for middle school students would be to form study groups giving each group the objectives list from such formal curriculum materials as Science—A Process Approach (SAPA), and Elementary School Science (ESS) to guide their thinking/selection/writing of specific objectives.

In deciding upon the actitivies and instructional methods, the first question that needs to be addressed is "How shall we go about it?" Tentative solutions that reflect individual and group interests and expertise is in order. Possible plans of action can be articulated in terms of the tentative solutions. A job analysis for the purposes of delegating and assuming responsibilities will address the second question of "Who will do each part of the work?" "Where might we do what needs to be done?" should be addressed by an inventory of skills and sources of information. Here is where we identify our writers, reporters, musicians, artists, chairpersons, researchers, etc. that reside in our class, school, and community-at-large. The question "When shall we do it?" should propel activity in the areas of securing, selecting, analyzing, and organizing the information/data into useable formats.

Finally, in evaluating what has been achieved, the focus is reflected in the question, "How can we evaluate our success in learning?" Here learning is broadly defined as both process and product. In a summative sense, we have the tasks of recording and recognizing the progress made by the individual student and the task of ascertaining the utility or practical applications of the project outcomes. Effort must also be expended for a formative (continuous) evaluation process that allows us to determine if the fulfillment of our plans involves some replanning and/or reassignment of individual and group responsibilities. This latter effort is facilitated by class discussions, written committee evaluations, and teacher observations.

Teacher-student planning is just one of many methods which may be used to help transescents gradually exercise more control over their lives in school. It reduces feelings of powerlessness and enhances self-esteem. It is worth trying.

While teacher-student planning will bring personal distinctiveness and meaning to the instruction, preplanning is necessary for a teacher to become a more effective participator in the program. One very effective way of preplanning is to construct resource units. Resource units place at the teacher's command an array of objectives, activities, resources and measuring devices for consideration during the teacher-student planning process. Combining resource units with a clear set of complimentary teacher and student roles (See Table 4.2) should lead one to the conclusion that both teachers and students assume responsibility for learning, with a most obvious attempt to help students develop a sense of control over their own environment - a condition which leads to the enhancement of both cognitive and affective development.

Table 4.2
The Role Definitions

Role	Teacher Behavior	Student Behavior
Planner	Prepares and collects material	Prepares and collects material
	Organizes items, spacing, sequence of materials	Organizes items, spacing, sequence of materials
	Constructs own materials	Constructs own materials
	Provides time and space for planning	Provides time and space for planning
	Writes or selects purposes and objectives	Writes or selects purposes and objectives
		Plans and consults with teacher and peers
Introducer	Presents materials to lead to inquiry and discussion	Student inquiry may lead to recycling of teacher role
	Selections appropriate material at appropriate time	Student follow-up
	Creates problematic situations	Creates problematic situations
Questioner	Asks question (or makes statement)	Responds
Sustainer	that stimulates (i.e.) open-ended divergent questions	Explores
		Asks
	Provides room for student opinion	Redirects
	Encourages explanation of different alternatives regarding problem	
	Redirects questions so as to maintain interaction	
Manager	Recognizes students	Recognizes students
	Makes announcements	Makes announcements
	Engages students in planning	Engages students in planning
	Keeps records	Keeps records
	Maintains order	Maintains order
	Provides optimum use of space, hardware, time (See Planner)	Provides optimum use of space, hardware, time (See Planner)
Rewarder	Consults with student (expresses intent and concern)	Evaluates self in reliable fashion
	Constructively criticizes student work	Progresses at a steady rate for self
	Evaluates and reports progress to parents	Shares information with peers, teacher, etc.
	Recognizes students (compliments, shares, etc.)	
	Allows time for all progress	

Our hunch is that by now the question arising in your mind is: "What is the role of subject matter in the problem-centered approach?" The action orientation of learning with the approach casts subject matter into a functional role. Subject matter is utilized according to its logical relationship to the problem being solved or need that is being met. To illustrate this point an analysis of sample activities from a problem unit entitled "Living In Our School" (Beane and Lipka, 1986) is offered for your consideration. This unit grew out of a classroom discussion about why young people must go to school for such a long period of their life. The discussion led to the formulation of the following objectives:

1. To identify the reasons why young people are required to go to school.
2. To describe what it takes to do well in school.
3. To identify the roles of various people in the school.
4. To investigate the reasons behind school and classroom rules.
5. To compare and contrast the school with the home.
6. To identify some of the problems faced by children in coming to school (p. 164, Beane and Lipka, 1986).

Two of the activities generated for these objectives were as follows:

(1) Students developed a list of the reasons why they think they have to come to school. They interviewed family members and adults in the school setting for additional reasons. Using the one-three-six technique the students rank ordered the reasons from most important to least important with a series of why statements to support their rankings of the reasons. The students then discussed the similarities and differences in the three sets of rankings.

(2) A set of procedures for welcoming new students to the school was developed. A committee was formed to carry out the procedures when necessary. They planned tours, introduced new students, and constructed packets of materials such as school rules, intermural offerings and the like.

The content functionally used in these activities consisted of at least the following:

CONTENT	ACTIVITY #1	ACTIVITY #2
Language Arts	*Listening* - interviews, group discussions *Speaking* - interviews *Reading* - interpreting interviews, list of reasons *Writing* - interview protocols, lists of reasons	*Listening* - committee work *Speaking* - conducting tours *Reading* - interpreting general school regulations, proofreading packets of materials *Writing* - tour guides, materials for packets
Social Studies	*Social Psychology* - general differences and similarities in the importance of school *Sociology* - importance of institutions (school) within our society; cooperation dynamics of group work	*Sociology* - school as a societal institution, cooperation, dynamics of group work
Mathematics	*Numeration* - use of ordinal numbers for ranking *Computation* - calculation of differences in rank	*Problem Solving* - determining number of packets needed *Computation* - costing out packets: per packet and total cost
Aesthetic Arts	*Visual Arts* - selection of media to display findings	*Visual Arts* - selection of paper, art work, typeface, etc. to produce appealing orientation packages

A unit of this type within a core of interdisciplinary program has students learning about many things (content) in school and, more importantly, learning about school itself with the goal of helping children to develop clear and confident self-perceptions with regard to school as a social institution.

46

HELPING THE LOW-STATUS LEARNER

For the teacher who is concerned about self-concept and esteem, perhaps no other case occupies more time than that of the very low-status learner. By this we mean concern for the young person who is never chosen to be on a team, to work in a small group, to participate in social activities, or to be a partner for a project.

At one time or another in our careers all of us have had such cases and worried about what we could do to help these young people to avoid derision from the group and become accepted by others. Often we tried to intervene in behalf of such learners by appointing them as captain of the team, assigning them to lead a group or, on a day when they are absent, lecturing the rest of the group on respect for individual dignity, concern for others, democracy, fair play, human rights, and the admirable qualities of the rejected individual. When this happens we are frequently struck by the apathy of the group, or worse yet their piercing looks which seem to put us in the same category as the low-status individual. Upon reflection we realized that we were virtually powerless to direct a group of learners to accept particular individuals. Still, we wonder how we can help.

In 1954 Louis Raths and his colleagues conducted a series of studies on status in groups of young people and its relation to classroom life. In explaining their findings we return again to the idea that learners have agendas of their own apart from the agendas of adults. Raths found that young people do establish clear status systems in peer groups and that they are based upon one or more factors from a set of categories including knowledge, skill, well-being, affection, influence and others. Humane and just or not, such systems are a common feature of groups and frequently contribute to a group's ability to get jobs done. Further, status is assigned by the group for reasons its members believe to be accurate and teachers cannot "talk" the group into changing its perception. In other words, teachers cannot assign status to individuals; only the group can do so. When such attempts are made the morale in the group tends to be low, not unlike the case of the new principal who assigns a low-status faculty member to chair an important committee.

Raths and his colleagues concluded that the way to work with low-status individuals was to help them earn their own way in the group. The process begins by the teacher being aware of the status system and working with it. This means supporting all learners, but giving the most visible support to the highest status individuals. Then, the teacher must try to find one or two things that the low-status individual knows or can do that might benefit the group. At this point the teacher can structure a group assignment or project which requires the low-status individual's knowledge or skill. For example, suppose such a learner is skilled in art. The teacher may ask a group to do a mural or to otherwise graphically illustrate a project. Needing skill in art work, the group may turn to our low-status individual for help. At this moment, the individual has a chance to demonstrate his or her skill, to help the group, and thus be seen in a new light. Similar examples could be described using access to needed information, skill with computers, ability to build models, or any other possible contribution to group efforts. Certainly there is no guarantee that one project will do the trick or that the elevated status will continue. But here is a place to start with a problem whose solution has long eluded us. Done in the context of continuous cooperative learning structures, this method might have long-lasting effects.

Beyond this we must remember that low-status individuals almost always have negative self-esteem. They have learned where they stand from experience and usually feel powerless to change things. It is not enough to say to them, "you are nice person, you should be accepted by the group." Individuals earn both high and low status by their actions. If an individual lacks social competence not only must we create opportunities to earn status, we must also help that person develop social skills. If an individual is incapable of leading groups, we must help him or her learn individual skills.

While being nice is a necessary ingredient for enhancing self-perceptions and social status, it is not enough. We must also be aware of status systems, structure opportunities for the group to re-assess its status assignments, and teach individuals the skills to earn their way in the group. Trying to pull rank on the group status structure will do little to help the low-status individual's self-esteem or place in the group and it will most certainly place our own standing in jeopardy.

Summary

Rearrangement of institutional features may go a long way toward enhancing self-perceptions in the middle school. Certainly such rearrangements are necessary, but alone they are not sufficient. Ultimately attention must be given to curriculum and teaching arrangements as well. Even where the content is rooted in academic subject areas, the use of techniques like cooperative learning and teacher-student planning coupled with a positive climate can influence self-concept and esteem in positive ways. But sooner or later the truly self-enhancing middle school must provide for some units which are actually based upon real needs, interests, problems and concerns of transcents.

Certainly there are critics of the kinds of approaches discussed in this chapter. Many of them are outside the middle level; high school academic specialists, federal and state officials who would turn the clock back to a classical academic education, and those in the general public and the media who are ill-informed. These people are clearly unaware of the nature of transescence and the need for unique schools at the middle level. We need to do a better job of educating such critics if efforts to reconsider curriculum and teaching are to have any chance for success.

However, additional work is also required within the middle school movement itself. Too many middle level educators seem convinced that the movement begins and ends with organizational re-structuring. They fail to see that it must eventually evolve in rearrangement of curriculum and teaching. Once taken, that step will bring us to the point where the middle schools more clearly reflect the goal of promoting mental health among transcents.

Chapter 5

The Self-Enhancing Middle School: The Kids Come First*

The field of education seems to live and die by the pendulum metaphor: professional fads come and go, and often come again. At each passing some resist the new direction while others jump on for the ride. Even now as we are in the midst of a swing toward more academic requirements and tougher standards there is talk about improving self-esteem of young people. Granted, some of that rhetoric has to do with the narrow view of self-perceptions as they relate to academic achievement or the idea that if we do something about self-esteem, youth will stop using drugs, getting arrested, getting pregnant, dropping out of school and otherwise causing trouble for themselves and us. Surely work on enhancing self-perceptions will make a mark in these areas.

However, our profession should realize that these reactive gestures are not really what makes this area of concern compelling. Rather it is the case that there are a few enduring and inevitable themes in education, one of which is the "humanness" of young people. In the end, when educators enhance self-concept and self-esteem, they are addressing the very core of transescents' lives. For that reason we cannot say strongly enough that this is not merely a matter of injecting a few activities into the school day or offering a semester elective in self-esteem. This is not a problem for easy, quick-fix solutions. It is not a place for commercial hucksterism where sideshow barkers call us in to see their fancy programs packaged in glossy covers. And, it is not a topic for false promises to learners where we say one thing for one period and then do something else for the remainder of the day.

Like everything else that is really worth doing, the matter of enhancing self-concept and self-esteem comes down to hard work over the long haul. It requires

---

* *"The Kids Come First" was the title of a poem written for the First Annual Seminar on the Young Adolescent at the University of Wisconsin/Platteville. The seminar, itself an affective happening, has grown from 66 participants in 1981 to over 700 in 1987 and the poem title has become the slogan for the Wisconsin Association for Middle Level Education.*

that we rethink the institutional features of school, even where these are rooted deeply in tradition. It requires that we reconsider our curriculum plans, thinking about self-perceptions each step along the way. It requires that we consciously reexamine our teaching behaviors and administrative procedures no matter how long they have been practiced. And it requires that we come to know transescents better than we do now. Only then will our profession have a chance to pull the enduring human needs of transescents out of the pendulum's path and make them part of a sustained and continuing effort to improve our middle schools.

In this last chapter we will try to sketch a portrait of a self-enhancing middle school and define the roles which must be played by principals, counselors, and teachers in such a school. Finally, we will consider the most difficult task ahead—developing advocacy for transescents outside the school.

PORTRAIT OF A SELF-ENHANCING MIDDLE SCHOOL

In this small volume we have described many parts of what we call a self-enhancing school. To see how they come together in a larger picture, let us imagine what such a school would be like if we were to visit one.

Our first impression comes from the physical appearance of the building, clearly this is a place that belongs to transescents and values their work. Hallways are lined with their artwork and trophy cases are filled with their projects.

The materials we are given (inevitably) include a statement of philosophy and objectives which focuses on the characteristics and needs of transescents rather than institutional goals. Prominently displayed among the objectives is one which speaks of improving self-esteem or helping transescents to feel good about themselves. The student handbook is written in a positive and encouraging tone; the statement of student expectations lists what they can and should do rather than stringing out a litany of "do nots." Further, as we are oriented to the school, we frequently hear references to self-concept and esteem, to the characteristics of transescence, and to their achievements both inside and outside the school.

As we tour the building we notice that people greet each other by name and often stop to inquire about how things are going. Our guide seems to know what many students do both in and out of school and mentions these things to them. The conversations we overhear are noticeably positive and free of sarcasm or harshness.

Looking in on classrooms we see many cases of discussions between teachers and students as well as small groups of students working together. While lecture and independent work are observed, they seem to be less frequently used than other patterns of teaching and learning. There is not much silence here since so many of the learners are actively solving problems and puzzles, dramatizing events, and otherwise making, building, and creating projects. Like the hallways, the classrooms are decorated with finished work and littered with that in progress.

Following our tour of the building we are invited to sit in on a meeting where a small group of teachers is discussing individual students who are experiencing difficulty in their classes. As each student is discussed comments are concentrated on things he or she has done well. As the teachers share what they know about the students, remarks are made about things going on inside and outside the school that might be causing stress or anxiety in their lives. Suggestions for help range from interviews with individual learners to ways that school pressure might be relieved. When instructional suggestions are made, they follow an analysis of

50

situations where the learner has previously enjoyed success. Obviously these teachers have positive regard for their students and want them to succeed. As the meeting breaks up, one teacher reminds the others that tomorrow they should finish planning the activities for their unit on getting along with others.

Following that meeting we are joined by a group of students who have been asked to tell us about their school. As they meet us and begin to answer our questions, they seem anxious to talk. One after another tells us about projects they have done, teachers they like, and activities they are involved in. One gives a lengthy description of service projects they have done in the community and invites us to see newspaper articles about them. Remarkably these students appear to be of diverse backgrounds, interests, skills and talents. When asked what they like most about this school they answer almost in chorus: "the teachers are nice to us . . . they like us."

Since it is time for lunch we are next invited to the school cafeteria. Unlike other schools we have visited teachers and students stand in line together—adults cannot simply cut in the front of the line. Naturally there is a fairly high noise level, but it is not chaotic. We do not hear cafeteria aides yelling at students. In fact, several teachers and the principal can be seen scattered around the room having lunch with groups of students. Those we join make room for us at their table and ask what we think of their school. We remark that it seems to be a nice place compared to some others we have been in. Hearing us describe these others as harsh places they look amazed. And when we say that the cafeteria food here is pretty good, the students tell us they help plan menus and take turns helping to clean up after lunch. Again we are struck by the realization that students in this school have the distinct impression that it belongs to them.

For the afternoon portion of our visit the schedule calls for sitting in on classroom activities. The first is an advisory program session. Here one teacher and about fifteen students are discussing a study of peer pressure. They have just completed a school-wide survey about social status and are analyzing results from questions about how cliques are formed and how their status is perceived. From the discussion it appears that the students themselves are representative of various cliques as they variously defend or challenge grounds for awarding status to groups. The teacher seems mostly to listen and ask questions that call for clarification of statements made by students. Toward the end of the period the group begins to discuss how they might disseminate results of their survey to other advisory groups in the school.

Next we sit in on a physical education class. Here the teacher is guiding students through a series of aerobic exercises which last for about twenty minutes. Then the group is joined by a science teacher who explains how such exercises benefit the cardio-vascular system. In the ensuing discussion students talk about their own lifestyles in terms of exercise, diet, and fitness. Finally the physical education teacher invites interested students to join the aerobics session scheduled during the school's daily elective activity program.

The last class we visit can hardly be called a class in the traditional sense. Actually it is a peer tutoring center where students may drop in to get help with assignments, projects, or study skills. The center is run by student volunteers

51

who have been trained in tutoring techniques. The room itself looks almost like a restaurant with its arrangement of small tables which seat two or three people. As we walk around the room we hear discussions ranging from how to construct a paper for a social studies class to how percentages are calculated. The one teacher in the room is working quietly on the side and is occasionally asked to help one or another tutoring team. Oddly enough while students are working and talking in close proximity they seem intent upon their work and pay little attention to what others are doing. In fact, our presence seems more like interference than an opportunity for distraction.

Our day ends with an invitation to join a school advisory council meeting. We quickly learn that those present represent teachers, administrators, counselors, non-certified personnel, parents, and students. Their agenda for today consists of discussing arrangements for orientation of new students who will come to the school in September. The initial comments are made by the students who outline fears, questions, and problems they faced when they came to middle school. Thereafter the whole group suggests various orientation activities including sending teams of teachers and students to visit each elementary school, organizing an orientation visit to the middle school for those who will be new students, setting up a big sister/brother program for the first few days in September, developing an information guide for new students and their parents, and more. A small steering committee is appointed to plan specific details and coordinate activities as they take place. Before concluding the meeting the group decides that at their next meeting they will review the school's program for orienting and introducing new students who transfer to the school.

As we review our visit it is clear that we have spent the day in a special kind of school. We have seen a place which is noticeably one for transescents. Their interests, needs, problems, and concerns have a visible place in curriculum plans. This school has a climate where personal and professional interactions are positive, humane, and supportive. People work cooperatively in planning, decision-making, and instruction. Students have opportunities to make connections with peers and with teachers who know them well. They also have many ways in which they may express themselves as well as develop a sense of self-worth. The teachers are nice, the activities are fun and a high premium is placed on learning together. All of these pieces are brought together in an overall emphasis on self-concept and esteem, a goal which serves as a unifying theme for a place where transescents come first. This, then, is a self-enhancing middle school.

The Principal's Role

Developing a self-enhancing middle school is not easy. Done successfully, the improvement of self-concept and esteem becomes a unifying theme not only in programs but in adult behavior as well. Over a period of years we have visited several schools which are lighthouse cases of this theme. During these visits we have observed certain behaviors by principals which seem to recur consistently and which lead us to believe that they are key ingredients. While we have no hard data to support our theory in this regard, these behaviors are so persistent as to be worth describing here.

In these schools the principals are con artists for kids. They know that the system is not necessarily set up to support transescents or their needs. Thus they find ways to manipulate the system to do so, or at least to neutralize its negative effects. For this reason, these principals are often at odds with other administrators, particularly those who are more interested in maintenance of order. These principals are also frequently late for meetings because they stop to talk with students and teachers or to help kids open their lockers.

The principals are also missionaries for the middle school. They are not just enthusiastic about making the school responsive to transescents; they are dedicated to the idea. They have a tendency to talk everyone else to death about unique kids and unique schools. When others ask them to be quiet, these principals are likely to stop talking, but also hand out some literature about middle schools and transescent learners.

The principals are no push-overs. They know a lot about transescent development and good middle schools. They know that the primary reward system for teachers resides in their relationships with their students and they do all they can to secure the resources and time that will assist teachers in strengthening these relationships. They know what has to be done to develop a good school and they work hard for it. They focus on enlightened philosophy not only when making big decisions, but also when making small, on-the-spot decisions while walking the halls. And when they are in the halls they know students' names and greet them that way. They know good things that students have done and make a point of mentioning them in casual conversation. When students cause conflict, these principals talk with them, sometimes at great length; corporal punishment is neither in their discipline repertoire nor their hearts. Ultimately, they want transescents to like themselves and those around them.

Clearly, this kind of principal behavior does not come easy, no matter how easy the good ones make it look. It would probably be much easier to simply keep a distance and maintain order. However, for these principals, the ones who are concerned with self-esteem, the ship does not have to run smoothly. In fact, they seem to fully recognize that constructive disequilibrium is as important in their development as it is in the lives of their students. They are not afraid to espouse the belief that the process of growing up is the process of making mistakes. They use their energies not to hide or cover up mistakes but rather to learn from mistakes and to fight for educational environments that will allow their students to learn from their efforts, interactions and mistakes.

The Counselor's Role

In our research we have asked transescents to tell us who influences their thinking about themselves or, in other words, who are the "significant others" in their lives. As it turns out, none has ever mentioned a guidance counselor in this role. This does not mean that no guidance counselor has ever helped a transescent; rather that young people in our studies have not perceived such professionals as significant influences. On the surface these data seem strange. After all, counselors are trained to provide personal and social support and serve in positions designated for that purpose. However, reality intrudes on this role.

The fact is that the guidance counselor/student ratio is such that counselors cannot possibly see individuals often enough to have the characteristic of significant others. Further, counselors are often cast in quasi-administrative roles. Time spent on scheduling and other similar tasks detracts from possible time with students.

Given these conditions, how can the guidance counselor play an effective part in enhancing self-concept and esteem? The key to answering this question is to imagine ways that counselors can *indirectly* participate by working through those who do see transescents frequently enough to be significant others (Beane, 1986). For example, techniques for interacting with learners about self-perception issues are part of the professional repertoire of most counselors, but not as often in that of others. So too is the design of activities and identification of useful materials in this area. Thus counselors can act as facilitators for other professionals and parents by teaching them interpersonal skills and assisting with curriculum planning.

Most counselors also know how to gather and interpret self-perception data and how to recognize symptoms of self-image problems. These too are not typically included in the preparation of other professionals and could be learned from counselors. In addition, guidance counselors can serve as sources of information about learners to improve the decision-making bases of both individual teachers and teams.

In terms of working directly with learners, counselors may create two settings. First, they can initiate group sessions on personal needs shared by learners. In this way they may have contact with larger numbers of transescents on a continuing and focused basis. Second, particularly in schools where advisory programs are set up to deal with common needs of transescents, counselors can work on a selective, referral basis with those who have specialized counseling needs.

Of course all of this depends upon a clear definition of the guidance counselor's role in the middle level school (Cole, 1981). Herein, perhaps, lies the real problem, larger even than carrying out effective roles. Job descriptions for counselors need to be clearly centered in counseling functions. The counselor who is a quasi-administrator cannot concentrate on transescent problems or needs. The counselor who is expected to act as a disciplinarian cannot also expect transescents to seek out his or her help on personal issues. On the other hand, the counselor who is given the time and responsibility for designing and implementing a guidance program may play a valuable role in efforts to enhance self-concept and esteem.

The Teacher's Role

Of all professional personnel in the school, teachers have the best chance to influence the self-perceptions of learners. This is for one rather simple reason: teachers have the kind of persistent, day-to-day contact with transescents that is necessary to become a significant other in their lives. It is also true that teachers are able to manipulate environmental factors which contribute to self-perceptions.

Most of us can recall, from one side of the desk or the other, times when the teacher let out an audible groan upon seeing a group of students for the first time. Likewise, we can probably remember a teacher telling us how hard the upcoming work would be and how much trouble previous students had with it or, worse yet, how this was the junior high school (or middle school) and the fun and games of the elementary school were over. These are examples of teacher expectations, one of the variables which is known to influence self-concept of ability. The examples mentioned were negative but teacher expectations certainly need not be so. In fact, if self-perceptions of transescents are to be enhanced, they must not be so. Teacher expectations are relayed to learners through verbal and non-verbal behavior embedded in ongoing interactions with students. Transescents in our research portrayed positive teacher expectations by citing "teachers who believe in us and praise us when we do good work." Put simply, persistent teacher expectations, no matter how subtle, are recognized by learners who over time begin to adopt them within their self-concepts and subsequently act them out. Where teachers believe in learners' ability to succeed, we tend to see learners who come to believe in themselves. And, where teachers structure learning opportunities to assure success, we tend to see progressively better achievement by learners and stronger self-esteem as well.

Beyond these two examples, teachers have the power to manipulate other areas related to self-perceptions that we have already discussed. They may become more sensitive to the characteristics and needs of transescents, offer learning experiences which address personal-social issues of transescents, provide more opportunities for working with peers, develop variability in materials and activities to support diversity of learner characteristics, and involve students in planning and evaluating learning experiences.

Furthermore, teachers may examine their own self-perceptions as both persons and as professionals. Criticisms of schools and teachers in the past decade progressively chipped away at our professional self-esteem. At social gatherings we are often reluctant to say that we are teachers. Also, as our profession has aged we have somehow lost some of the commitment and enthusiasm we had as young teachers. Yet we know that teacher self-concept often rubs off on learners. Granted we are often discouraged by poor morale in our school settings and debilitating behavior by some administrators. At some point though, we must look within ourselves to see how morale and self-esteem can be improved. And, teachers must insist on environments which enhance their self-perceptions, volunteering where necessary to work for their development.

Finally, it is necessary to note that some teachers shy away from the area of self-perceptions because they think that personal-social growth of transescents is the responsibility of someone else or because they do not know how to go about dealing with such concerns. At the beginning of this monograph, three reasons were explained for attending to self-perceptions in the middle school, one historical, one moral, and one research based. Somewhere in these three reasons there should be an argument that persuades even the most reluctant among us to take action. However, teachers are not psychologists trained to deal with specialized counseling needs of youth. That is what counselors and other referral services are for. Nor are teachers solely responsible for the personal-social growth of transescents. Others both inside and outside the school have roles to play. On the other hand, teachers do have some responsibility in this area and it is summed up eloquently by Louis Raths in his work *Meeting the Needs of Children* (1972):

What about those children who are "crying inside"? Some of them want love or praise or friends so very, very much, and they can only think about what they are lacking. They cannot hear us when we try to teach. Until we try to meet some of their needs, we shall probably be unsuccessful in our teaching efforts. And if we are able to satisfy some of these needs, just think of what a difference it will make in the life of the child. For him, the whole world will probably become a different place, a happier, more secure, more trusting and trustworthy place . . . I want to say again that it is your professional job to help children to grow, to learn, to mature. The meeting of needs is not your sole responsibility. But, if unmet needs are getting in the way of a child's growth and development, his learning and his maturing, I insist that it is your obligation to try to meet his needs. I say that with conviction. I believe it from the bottom of my heart. And so do you, probably. I'm pretty sure that if a child needed glasses you would take some steps to help meet that need. And if a child had some difficulty in hearing you might make many efforts to help him to learn. And so also with unmet emotional needs.

Beyond the School

As we come toward the close of the 1980's it is clear that the middle school movement of the past two decades has been a significant episode in twentieth century education. Admittedly the impetus for change at the local level was and still usually is overcrowding or low enrollment, building plans, and other administrative problems. However, at some point the local middle level educators have typically explored the need for change in both organizational and curriculum rearrangements to better fit with the characteristics of transescence. So we have seen the virtual reconstruction of an institution; from the junior version of the high school to the modern middle level school.

Among other things, one typically finds that such schools have some form of interdisciplinary teaming, block schedules, advisory programs, exploratory electives, and so on. When you change the schedule, the staffing pattern, the philosophy, and the curriculum, you are truly changing the sacred cows and the substance of the school. And that is no simple trick.

Yet this kind of change, fundamental as it may be, is still not enough. To improve the quality of life for transescents during school is a wonderful thing. But surely the movement means more than this. If we really care about these young people and if we also realize that their life outside the school is not all that it should be, then we must find a way to make that lever which has changed the school long enough to move the society at large toward a more supportive role for transescents.

This statement does not deny the many efforts by middle level educators to educate and inform parents. It does, however, call for greater action beyond the school. It means that we must not only invite parents into the schools, but visit them in their homes and organize parent workshops in neighborhood centers. It means that we must involve pediatricians, social workers, local government officials, law enforcement personnel, media personnel, clinical psychologists, business officials, and others in our talk about transescents and their needs. It means that we must put transescents in touch with special community projects which could benefit from their altruism and thus cast them in more favorable roles. It means speaking out in support of transescents in informal conversations, in letters to the editor, and in public meetings. It means pressuring local communities to develop programs and set aside space for transescents to come together outside the school. In short, it means standing up for transescents outside the school with the same enthusiasm and commitment we have demonstrated on the inside in an attempt to build networks of advocacy across our society.

Earlier in this volume we described a moral line of reasoning for attending to self-concept and esteem of transescents. We suggested that for many of them the middle school has become a kind of Maginot Line in their lives, a last place where they might find a group of adults with continuing interest in their welfare. But this need not necessarily be so. Over time, through the kinds of action just described, we might find whole communities becoming safe, sane, and secure places for transescents. Without such action the middle school will continue to mostly stand alone, happy with its internal success, but frustrated in its desire for a better overall quality of living for youth.

The matter of turning our attention beyond the school is filled with exasperating probabilities. Meetings will be sparsely attended. Newspaper articles will be buried in the back pages. Public officials will have too many items on their agendas. People will simply be too busy to talk, let alone act. But, if we persist and take risks, if we begin to affect even a few, maybe the word will spread and the movement will grow. And perhaps in the long haul what we want for transescents in the community at large and inside the schools as well will be secured in the expectations of our society. Then a book about enhancing self-concept and esteem in transescence may be written not as a set of recommendations, but as a description.

Appendix A

An Illustrative Unit: The Family of Peers

Objectives

1. To analyze reasons why peers are important.
2. To identify ways in which the peer group influences attitudes, behavior, and values.
3. To compare and contrast peer values with those of adults.
4. To identify reasons why friends are chosen.
5. To analyze the clique and status structure in the school.
6. To compare and contrast the values and standards of various cliques.
7. To describe personal contributions one makes to the peer group.

Content (for the teacher to use in planning with students)

1. One characteristic of older childhood and transescence is emergence of the peer group. For some dimensions of self-perceptions (e.g., dress, body build, language), feedback from the peer group becomes more influential than that of parents.
2. Acceptance by peers is probably the most preoccupying motive for behavior of older children and transescents.
3. The standards of the peer group often conflict with those of adults, including teachers. This conflict is typical for the age group, but often leads adults to react harshly or angrily.
4. Developing social connections with peers is one of the initial steps toward developing emotional independence from parents and other adults.
5. Even though acceptance by peers is important, older children and transescents often need the assurance of adult support on highly emotional issues.
6. Individuals are often so immersed in peer group dynamics that they are not clear about the degree to which they are being influenced by the peer group.
7. The overall peer group in older childhood and transescence typically divides into smaller cliques, each one with its own set of specific standards. Competition among cliques is often acute, and even though they are accepted in one clique, individuals may wish they were members of another.

Activities

1. Develop a series of sociograms for a group of peers. Base each one on a different idea:
   a. Whom would each person like to do a school project with?
   b. Whom would each person choose as a partner for an athletic event?
   c. Whom would each person like to have as a best friend?

   For each sociogram, discuss with a small group the reasons why people were chosen. Also look for differences in choices among the sociograms and discuss why different choices were made for different events or ideas.
2. Develop a list of cliques among the peer group in the school. For each one, cite the outstanding ideas that the clique has about behavior, attitudes, values, and the like. Also identify how one is accepted into the clique and under what conditions a member might be rejected. Compare the analysis with others.
3. Prepare a skit or play that dramatizes a major school event. Develop characters on the basis of caricatures or stereotypes of cliques.
4. Describe events, language, or behavior that are generally approved and disapproved by the peer group.
5. In a small group, develop a series of "Ann Landers" type responses to typical problems of your age group. For example:
   a. How does one resolve a fight with a good friend?
   b. How should one explain to friends that he or she has been grounded by parents a few days before a major social event?
   c. What does one do if he or she is at a party where drugs or alcohol are being used and he or she doesn't want to use them?
6. Role play conflict events among peers. Try to use such interpersonal techniques as reflective listening, paraphrasing, and clarifying responses.
7. Develop a list of the behavior standards, attitudes, and values of your own clique. Note those that you have initiated. Rank standards in order of priority to the group and to yourself. Think of one or more issues on which you would take a stand against your clique.

Resources

About Me (booklet with activities, charts, and ideas for self-evaluation). Encyclopedia Britannica Educational Corporation.

Bread and Butterflies. Agency for Instructional Television (series of fifteen programs designed specifically for emerging adolescents).

The Family You Belong To; The Friends You Make; The Person You Are (booklets with activities for analyzing self and environment. New York: Follet Publishing Co.

Living With Others (cassettes). South Holland, Ill.: Wilson Corporation.

Physical and Emotional Targets for Teenagers (cassettes and filmstrips). Q-ED Productions (a division of Cathedral Films, Inc.).

Self-Incorporated. Agency for Instructional Television (series of fifteen programs designed specifically for emerging adolescents).

Measuring Devices

Since the objectives in this unit plan are directed toward enhancing self-perception, work done by students should be accepted unconditionally. However, the teacher should be alert to the following kinds of criteria in observing and reviewing student work:

1. Does the student evidence understanding of the peer group as an influence?
2. Does each student feel accepted by at least one or two peers?
3. Are the analyses of clique structures and clique standards accurate and complete?
4. Does the student seem willing to accept others, especially those who are not particularly "best" friends?
5. Are cliques based on generally pro-social values and standards. If not, are students aware of this?
6. Do individuals perceive themselves as contributing members of their cliques or are they simply followers?
7. Are students developing skills in constructive interpersonal communications? Are they evident in activities other than role-playing, such as those that take place outside the classroom?

Appendix B

Transescents Talk About Themselves In School: What Seventh Graders Told Us

During the initial planning of this book we agreed to continue our "modus operandi" of asking young people to involve themselves in our work. Each of us went to the middle school in our home community and offered a group of seventh graders the following letter:

Kids:

I am co-authoring a short book about kids your age for the National Middle School Association. It will be read by teachers, administrators, guidance counselors, and people who are going to college to learn to be teachers. I would like to know what you think these people need to know about you. That is, what "things" should these people know about you so that they may work better with you in a middle school setting.

By "things" I mean:

1. Things you think about in school.
2. Things you talk about in school with friends, teachers and others.
3. Things that make you feel good about yourself in school.
4. Things that make you feel bad about yourself in school.
5. The changes you are going through at this time in your life.
6. Any other things you think these people ought to know.

Thank you very much for your assistance.

The young people were allowed to discuss these questions in small groups and prepare a small group written response to each of the questions. What follows is a verbatim (minus duplicates) transcript of their responses. We offer you this full list for a number of reasons.

Perhaps you are presently not in a position to work directly with this age group - such a listing can give you an overview of this age group.

Perhaps you are now working with this age group and you wish to see how your students' responses to the questions stack up against the students we talked to for this book.

Perhaps you may wish to use the student comments as an informal checklist in evaluating your formal and informal curriculum for its attention to affective development in general and self-concept/self-esteem in particular.

If you find other ways to use the student comments please drop us a line and share your thinking.

For whatever assistance they provide - here are the *verbatim* comments:

Question #1: **Things you think about in school.**
How bad I would get in trouble if I would get a bad grade.
How he hates it when they assign homework because work should stay at school and not on our free time.
Sex
Opposite sex
Sports
Music
Getting our work completed, and turn in is a daily task.
Talking about what kind of bikes we have.
Trying to get other people in trouble.
Girls
Different subjects
School Dances
Teachers
What to do after school.
Homework
Sometimes it's very boring & we need some excitement.
Some things should be explained more than others, they (teachers) need to be coaches rather than giving you the answers right off.
Boyfriends
Weekly parties
Nuclear War
Mommer Khadafe
problems w/in the family
worry about my peers feel about us and how they well treat us.
When I have a dentist or doctor appointment, I worry about it.
Family worries - such as sickness, death, bills, etc.
When classes get boring, we like to sit & daydream about our boyfriends & our future.
Cheerleading
Band tryouts
Worry about tests
Worry about weight
How our hair and clothes look
How big our feet are
How we smell
Worry about our reputations.
End of the hour or day
School

Future
Rock groups
friends
parties
life
movies/T.V.
What we look like
Summer vacation/Summer
Clothing
Problems
Fridays
Parents
Better food than school food
Comebacks when in fights
home
getting good grades
being late for class
what time it is
getting out of school
failing
detention
passing
going to the library
telling jokes
hunting
seeing a movie in class
fights after school
brothers and sisters
movies
books
summer
gymnastics
birthdays
getting work done
what friends are doing

Question #2: **Things you talk about in school with friends, teachers and others.**

sports
girls
classwork
bad jokes
fights
who you hate
homework
what you got on tests

people stealing from lockers
parties
grades
Libya
World War III
school work
wrestling
movies
bikes
fishing
sports
family
work
having fun
staying home
Dr. Ruth
sex
Khadafy
problems
how to do work
boys
Music
problems
Friday night
what you did over the weekend
boyfriends
making up work
friends
helping each other with homework
teachers (good and bad)
food and dieting
parents
vacation plans
Hobbies
Interests
Girl friends
Cars
Bleep
Rock-n-Roll
Anything
Homework problems
Triumphs
We're willing to talk to really good friends about most problems.
We feel that we can talk more freely to friends.
Nuclear War
Personal matters

Prayer
Debateable, important issues such as animal lab experiments (pro/con?)
What we got on a certain test
How we feel about the opposite sex.
We like to talk about Khadafy and his "Death Line"
Our pets
Personal feelings
Travel
Concerts
How we feel about the latest trends
Rules
Future of our country
Abortion (debate)
Morals
Next year
Make-up/acne
Hair styles
Tests
Each other
Normal gossip
Khaddafy
Assignments
Why we were tardy

Question #3: **Things that make you feel good about yourself in school.**
Girls
friends
Knowing that school is almost out
Getting good grades on tests & grade cards
Compliments
Helping others
Others helping you
Meeting new friends
When friends don't keep secrets from you.
When teachers take the time to explain things to you.
When people say Hi when you walk down the hall.
When upper classmen are nice to me.
When teachers compliment me on my work and writing.
When people tell me that I look nice or they like my clothes.
When a really gorgeous guy starts flirting with me.
When I bring my headset.
When I break school rules.
When I wear good-smelling perfume.
Knowing that it is almost the end of the school day.
Eating cinnamon rolls during lunch.
Saying you look nice

Today
Saying thanks/Compliments
Opposite sex talking to you
Solving problems
No homework
Fun classes
Nice teachers
friends
having a girlfriend
when you beat up your enemy
passing
being popular
lunch
3:00
having a boyfriend
making up with a friend that you have just been in a fight with
the teacher calls on you when you have the answer
when you get applauded by classmates
when a cute boy asks you out
when the bell rings to go home
seeing fine-looking boys
candy
study hall
when certain teachers aren't here
some teachers
the way you look
being away from family
staying out of trouble

Question #4: **Things that make you feel bad about yourself in school.**
If I made a bad grade.
Girls
Lunch
Flunking a test.
Friends talking about you behind your back.
Getting an 8th. hour.
Not being able to get your locker open.
When someone makes you look & feel foolish.
Being tardy
Getting in trouble
When someone is mad at you.
When people talk bad about people you like.
When people back-stab.
When somebody is mad & won't tell you why.
When teachers teasingly put you down.
When people put me down.

When my friends and I get into fights.
When people look at me like I'm a real geek.
When teachers give dirty looks.
When people tell me to go away.
Goting to T.A.
When you get a bad grade from a teacher just because he/she doesn't like
    you.
People criticizing.
Teachers yelling.
Getting in trouble/talking.
Dirty looks.
Two faced people.
When girls/boys break up with you.
When your teacher gets made at you for talking in class.
When everyone is on you.
When you can't trust your friends.
When your teachers don't like you for other friends/relatives who act or
    have acted bad in their class.
Not having friends.
Not getting homework done.
Being in school.
Getting beat up.
Detention
Homework
Getting in trouble with a teacher or principal.
Losing a friend.
Kids
Getting beat up
If your friends have drugs.
Not catching fish the day before.
Detention
In school suspension.
When you borrow, then lose something.
When an ugly boy asks you out.
Social studies and math class
When you can't do something in gym and get hollered at.
When you lose all your friends.
When you ask fine boys out and they say no.
Out-of-school suspension.
Eating school food
When you come to school sick.
When teachers don't like the way you look.

Question #5: **The changes you are going through at this time in your life.**
Friends
Interests

Get moody sometimes
Voice change
taller
Heavery more
emphasis on looks
maturing mentally & physically
Different personality
Becoming more responsible
Confusion in deciding between kids or mature young adults.
Our parents treating us our age.
Different parts of our body are beginning to change into men & women.
We are starting to have emotional & physical attraction for the opposite sex.
We are beginning to understand what we must do in life and who we want
    to be.
We've started to understand how quickly time passes.
We also understand that you don't live forever.
We are beginning to have more respect for our elders, but by the same
    token we want to rebel.
Puberty
Acne
We're growing up.
We're learning to feel love & recognize it.
We no longer have all the answers therefore we always feel like we're
    missing something.
None of us want to be grownup, so we fight it. I suppose thats a big reason
    we're depressed alot.
More responsibilities.
More arguments with friends & parents.
Start smoking.
Start drinking.
Your sex life
Clothes
Start chewing tobacco
Trying to be good.
Different girls.
Big decisions (smoking, drugs, snuff, alcohol)
Getting braces or getting them off.
Facts of Life.
Being picked on by older kids.
Dealing drugs.
Meeting different people.
Going places with boys.
Wearing new clothes styles.
Meeting different people.
New hairdos.
Writing neater

More studying and harder work
Classes in different rooms
Peer pressure to do drugs, alcohol, etc.
Making new friends.
Final exams
New ways of punishing you in junior high (detention, suspension)
To say yes or no to your boyfriend.

Question #6: **Any other things you think these people ought to know.**
I wish the teachers wouldn't assign homework on Fridays.
We do not enjoy school.
We do enjoy fights.
That seventh graders are pretty easy to get along with if you give us a
   chance.
Why can't we be treated like a Junior High?
We're tired of being treated like little kids.
We're teenagers & if we're expected to act like teenagers we want to be
   treated that way.
We need more experience in real life than in our sheltered world.
If computers are our future that's what we need training in.
We think having Middle Schools is a good idea.
It gives us a chance to experiment & be successful with changing classes &
   having lots of teachers.
We feel that by the time we are in 7th. & 8th. grade we should have a little
   more freedom.
We would like to have competition in sports like high schools.
Teachers should not take their bad moods out on kids & if they are sick &
   not feeling well *go home.*
We don't need to listen to teachers gripe, scream, look in pain, or start
   crying or having a nervous breakdown - we're moody enough - we don't
   need the bull.
We wish people would just get off our backs.
We understand the part about responsibility but seems like adults are
   constantly on our case.
What makes it worse is that they think we're really little kids.
I don't understand why they can't simply talk to us in normal voices instead
   of yelling & screaming like wild banshees!
You'd think that teachers would have enough respect for us not go give us
   real long lectures about the simplest things.
We've heard them all before!
For teachers not to blow up.
Wish more teachers would trust us more.
They should make the classes more fun.
For teachers to encourage us to try harder & get better grades.
For teachers to let us listen to the radio in class.
More time for changing classes.

We're sneaky

We are intelligent.

Lunch time should be longer.

Teachers should know some kids take school seriously and some don't.

Teachers should know some kids need extra help and they should spend more time explaining things to them.

If students are forgetful sometimes teachers shouldn't yell at them or make them stay after.

Teachers shouldn't embarrass students.

Facts of life.

Peer pressure.

More get-togethers.

Don't get mad at us unless they know for sure that we did it.

Teachers should not be so hard on us.

When they want you to be quiet use proper language instead of saying shut up.

Teachers should realize that they push students too fast.

Teachers should realize that no one can learn everything.

They should leave their family problems at home instead of bringing them to school and being mean to us.

We should have a longer summer vacation.

Teachers should make our finals easier.

Let us chew gum.

Don't take things away from us.

They should not be ble to grab our arms and hurt us when they get mad.

For teachers to let us listen to the radio in class.

School should be shortened.

We should be able to have a little fun in study hall.

School shouldn't be like prison, we are free people.

Our thanks to these young people
who helped us

Molly Beezley	Eric Cameron
Scott Blakemore	Brian Fairfield
Neil Bryan	William Hollamby
Stephanie Creel	Catherine Hoy
Nick Gray	Karri Johnson
Janice Griffiths	Aaron Kreydt
Talaina Helton	Todd Lovell
Heather Henderson	Julie Mancini
Dennis Kester	Daniel Martin
Andy Kraner	Jeanett Morrison
Jennifer La Barr	Kimberly Owens
Jennifer Lipka	Amy Reynolds
Scott Massoth	Kimberly Rybicki
Catherine Minor	James Stitt
Keri Randall	Jeffrey Thompson
Chris Rourk	Tammy Schoepflin
Robbie Schlemmer	Aledia Weatherall
Stacy Scifers	Richard Williams
Veronica Snider	James Woodring
Sheila Babb	Scott Wright
Allyson Batt	Lori Wright
April Belleisle	George Van Cleaf
Michael Brandow	James Ziegler

and to their teachers
Linda Barberich and Robert Sherman

Appendix C

Self-Assessment Checklists[*]

CHECKLIST I

Characteristic Attitudes and Behaviors of Teachers Who Enhance Self-Perceptions

	YES	NO
Do I accept students as human beings, regardless of their background?	___	___
Do I enjoy the diversity of individual differences in a group?	___	___
Do I provide opportunities for students to pursue personal interests?	___	___
Am I sensitive to the group's status system and do I help individuals achieve status in the group?	___	___
Do I attempt to learn about student lives outside the classroom?	___	___
Do I provide many opportunities for interaction and cooperation?	___	___
Do I involve students in planning and evaluating activities and projects?	___	___
Do I avoid equating the learners' work with their self-worth?	___	___
Do I respect the personal dignity of students?	___	___
Do I encourage students to think about themselves?	___	___
Do I help students to find personal meaning in ideas and concepts?	___	___
Do I encourage parents or guardians to be active and constructive in children's education?	___	___
Do I encourage students to help each other in learning and problem solving?	___	___
Am I happy to be involved in teaching?	___	___

*From Beane, James A. & Lipka, Richard P. *Self-Concept, Self-Esteem, and The Curriculum* New York: Teachers College Press, 1986

72

Do I encourage students to pursue ideas about which I am not knowledgeable? ___ ___

Do I trust students to carry out projects responsibly? ___ ___

Do I have positive and realistic expectations of students? ___ ___

Do I seek new and worthwhile ideas for improving teaching? ___ ___

Do I speak out on behalf of children and youth in the school and community? ___ ___

Am I concerned about the quality of living for children and youth in society? ___ ___

Do I volunteer to work with students outside the classroom? ___ ___

Do I provide a variety of resources for classroom use? ___ ___

Do I encourage students to challenge others' ideas and to seek support for their own? ___ ___

Do I feel secure when students challenge teacher ideas? ___ ___

Do I recognize the influence of various pressures on students and their effect of learning? ___ ___

Am I willing to share personal feelings with students? ___ ___

Am I flexible; willing to revise plans as needed? ___ ___

Do I help students to learn about their personal backgrounds and possible futures? ___ ___

Do I treat student mistakes or failure at a task as an opportunity for new learning and growth? ___ ___

Am I willing to share ideas with other teachers? ___ ___

Do I recognize the power of self-perceptions in learning? ___ ___

Do I have patience in working with learning difficulties? ___ ___

Do I purposefully plan activities at which students can succeed? ___ ___

Do I recognize and use the community as a source of teaching and learning? ___ ___

Am I willing to try new approaches and ideas even though some risk is involved? ___ ___

CHECKLIST II

Characteristic Attitudes and Behaviors of Teachers
Who Hinder Positive Learner Self-Perceptions

	YES	NO
Do I believe students are "evil" and irresponsible?	___	___
Do I label individuals with personal perceptions of the group?	___	___
Do I have low expectations for students and believe they will fail no matter how hard they try?	___	___
Do I believe I am the source of all worthwhile knowledge?	___	___
Do I believe students should concentrate only on those ideas that are of interest to the teacher?	___	___
Do I feel that students should be able to ignore personal/social problems when working on cognitive tasks?	___	___
Do I personally plan all learning activity?	___	___
Am I reluctant to deviate from prepared curriculum plans?	___	___
Do I equate school success with personal self-worth of students?	___	___
Do I think learning difficulties are the fault of anything or anybody but me?	___	___
Do I force students to compete for rewards?	___	___
Do I refuse to involve students in ideas about which I am unsure or unknowledgeable?	___	___
Do I believe last year's curriculum plans are suitable for this and succeeding years?	___	___
Do I assume that learning, growing, and developing take place on a constant continuum?	___	___
Do I wish that I could get out of teaching?	___	___
Do I refuse to accept students' challenges of my ideas or opinions?	___	___
Am I sure that I know what all students need?	___	___
Do I have no interest in the personal interests of students?	___	___
Do I believe that classroom misbehavior is sure to lead to adult failure and illegal behavior?	___	___
Do I believe that students will not learn unless motivated by me?	___	___
Do I believe maintenance of order is the first condition of learning?	___	___
Do I confuse submission of students with willingness to learn?	___	___

Do I use punitive punishment, humiliation, and sarcasm in dealing with students?   ____ ____

Do I wish students would act like adults rather than young people?   ____ ____

Do I believe parents should not help their children with school-related learning?   ____ ____

Do I equate student cooperation with cheating?   ____ ____

Do I make all decisions about curriculum plans?   ____ ____

Do I reserve the exclusive right to evaluate student work?   ____ ____

Do I think education is preparation only for future living?   ____ ____

CHECKLIST III

Characteristics of the Self-Enhancing School

	YES	NO

Is the idea of enhancing self-perceptions a high priority in our school? ____ ____

Do students have a say in what happens in our school? ____ ____

Do we avoid stereotyping students? ____ ____

Do we emphasize cooperation rather than competition? ____ ____

Do we avoid the idea that some students will fail no matter how hard they try? ____ ____

Do we do whatever possible to assure success for students? ____ ____

Do we make an effort to help students earn status with their peers? ____ ____

Do we make arrangements for peer tutoring as well as interaction with younger and older persons? ____ ____

Do we make arrangements to teach parents how to interact and work with their children in constructive ways? ____ ____

Do our curriculum plans make provisions for enhancing self-perceptions? ____ ____

Do our school goals include clean and direct statements that commit us to enhancing self-perceptions? ____ ____

Does each school level have general objectives committing it to enhancing self-perceptions? ____ ____

Does our school program offer opportunities for students to learn about themselves? ____ ____

Does our school have established communications with community agencies that supply support services for children and youth? ____ ____

Do we make use of the problems and needs approaches? ____ ____

Do we use issues for present lives of students as organizing centers for curriculum plans? ____ ____

Do students participate in making classroom decisions?' ____ ____

Are a variety of activities and materials available from which students may make choices? ____ ____

Do we observe and record changes in student self-perceptions? ____ ____

Do we discuss changes in self-perception with students and parents? ____ ____

Do students have an opportunity to evaluate themselves?   ____ ____

Do our curriculum plans offer opportunities for students to
improve their present lives?   ____ ____

REFERENCES

Alessi, S. & Toepfer C. (1971). Guidance in the middle school. *Dissemination Services on the Middle Grades, 1,* 1-6.

Alexander, W. et al. (1968) *The emergent middle school,* New York: Holt, Rinehart, and Winston.

Allport, G. W. (1955). *Becoming.* New Haven, CT: Yale University Press.

Anderson, V.E. (1956) *Principles and procedures of curriculum development.* New York: Ronald Press.

Beane, J.A., and Lipka, R.P. (1980). Self-concept and self-esteem: A construct differentiation. *Child Study Journal,* 10, 1-6.

Beane, J. (1986). The self-enhancing middle grade school. *The School Counselor, 33,* 189-195.

Beane, J.A. & Lipka, R.P. (1986) *Self-concept, self-esteem, and the curriculum.* New York: Teachers College Press.

Brinthaupt, T.M. & Lipka, R.P. (1985). The high school years: A view of adolescent self concept and self-esteem. Paper presented at the Annual Meeting of the Mid-Western Educational Research Association, Chicago, Illinois.

Brookover, W.; Thomas S.; & Paterson, A. (1964). Self concept of ability and school achievement. *Sociology of Education, 37,* 271-278.

Brookover, W. (1965). *Self-concept of ability and school achievement.* East Lansing Michigan: Office of Research and Publications, Michigan State University.

Bryan, T. & Bryan, J. (1986). Self-concepts and attributions of the learning disabled. *Transescence, 14,* 33-40.

Cole, C. (1981). Middle school guidance: A shared responsibility. *Dissemination Services on the Middle Grades, 13,* 1-4.

Cooley, C.H. (1902). *Human nature and the social order.* New York: Charles Scribner's.

Coopersmith, S. (1967). *The antecedents of self-esteem.* San Francisco: W. H. Freeman.

Diebert, J. & Hoy, W. (1977). Custodial high schools and self-actualization of students. *Educational Research Quarterly, 2,* 24-31.

Dewey, J. (1902). *The child and the curriculum.* Chicago: University of Chicago Press.

Eisner, E. (1969). Instructional and expressive educational objectives: Their formation and use in curriculum. In W. J. Popham, et al., *Instructional Objectives.* Chicago: Rand McNally.

Elkind, D. (1967). Egocentrism in adolescence. *Child Development, 38,* 1025-34.

Epstein, S., (1973). The self-concept revisited: Or a theory of a theory. *American Psychologist, 28,* 404-416.

Findley, W. & Bryan, M. (1975) *The pros and cons of ability grouping.* Bloomington, In: Phi Delta Kappa

Fraenkel, J.R. (1980). *Toward a more comprehensive model of value education.* Paper presented at the Annual Meeting of the American Educational Research Association, Boston, MA.

Gergen, K.J. (1971). *The concept of self.* New York: Holt, Rinehart and Winston.

Gilman, F. (1984). Teacher self-perceptions and their perceptions of student characteristics: A selected review of recent literature. *Journal of Classroom Interaction, 19,* 9-11.

Gordon, C. (1968). Self-conceptions: Configurations of content. In C. Gordon & K. J. Gergen (Eds), *The self in social interaction.* New York: Wiley.

Gruhn, W. & Douglas, H. (1947). *The modern junior high school.* New York: Ronald Press.

Harmin, M. et al. (1973). *Clarifying values through subject matter: Applications for the classroom.* Minneapolis: Winston.

Hedin, D. & Conrad, D. (1980). Study proves hypotheses and more. *Synergist, 9,* 8-14.

James, M. (1986). *Adviser-advisee programs: Why, what and how.* Columbus, OH: National Middle School Association.

Johnson, D.W., Johnson, R.T., Holubec, E.J. & Roy, P. (1984) *Circles of learning: Cooperation in the classroom.* Alexandria, VA: Association of Supervision and Curriculum Development.

Kelley, E.C. (1962). The fully functioning self. In A.W. Combs (Ed.), *Perceiving, behaving, becoming: A new focus for education.* Washington, D.C.: Association for Supervision and Curriculum Development.

Krug, E.A. (1950) *Curriculum planning.* New York: Harper Brothers.

Lipka, R.P., Beane, J.A., & Ludewig, J.W. (1980). *Self-concept/esteem and the curriculum.* Paper presented at the Annual Conference of the Association for Supervision and Curriculum Development, Atlanta, GA.

Lipka, R.; Beane, J.; & O'Connell, B. (1985). *Community service projects: Citizenship in action.* Bloomington, IN: Phi Delta Kappa.

Lipka, R.P., & Brinthaupt, T.M. (1986). Self-concept/self-esteem indicators of the transescent: Implications for educators. *Transescence, 14.* 18-32.

Mead, G.H. (1934). *Mind, self and society.* Chicago, IL: University of Chicago Press.

Melton, G. (1984). The junior high school: Successes and failures. In J. Lounsbury (Ed.), *Perspectives: Middle school education, 1964-1984.* Columbus, OH: National Middle School Association.

Newmann, F. & Rutter, R. (1983). *The effects of high school community service programs on student's social development.* Report to the National Institute of Education. Madison, WI: Wisconsin Center for Educational Research.

Lounsbury, J. & Vars, G. (1978). *A curriculum for the middle school years.* New York: Harper.

Purkey, W. (1970). *Self concept and school achievement.* Englewood Cliffs, NJ: Prentice-Hall.

Purkey, W. (1978). *Inviting school success. A self concept approach to teaching and learning.* Belmont, CA: Wadsworth.

Purkey, W. & Strahan, D. (1986). *Positive discipline: A pocketful of ideas.* Columbus, OH: National Middle School Association.

Raths, L. (1954). Power in small groups. *The Journal of Educational Sociology, 28,* 97-103.

Raths, L. E. (1998). *Meeting the needs of children: Creating trust and security.* Troy, NY: Educator's International Press

Rogers, C.R. (1951). *Client-centered therapy.* Boston: Houghton Mifflin.

Rosenberg, M. (1979). *Conceiving the self.* New York: Basic Books.

Slavin, R. (1981). Synthesis of research on cooperative learning. *Educational Leadership, 38,* 655-660.

Snygg, D. & Combs, A.W. (1949). *Individual behavior: A new frame of reference for psychology.* New York: Harper and Brothers.

Stevenson, C. (1986). *Teachers as inquirers: Strategies for learning with and about early adolescents.* Columbus, OH: National Middle School Association.

Sullivan, H.S. (1953). *The interpersonal theory of psychiatry.* New York: Norton.

Vars, G.F. (1987). *Interdisciplinary teaching in the middle grades, why and how.* Columbus, OH: National Middle School Association.

Willover, D. & Jones, R. (1963). When pupil control becomes an institutional theme. *Phi Delta Kappan, 45,* 107-107.

Wylie, R. (1961). *The self-concept: A critical survey of pertinent research literature.* Lincoln, NE: University of Nebraska Press.

Wylie, R. (1979). *The self-concept: Theory and research on selected topics* (Vol. 2). Lincoln, NE: University of Nebraska Press.